Freire and Drama

FREIRE IN FOCUS

Series editors: Greg William Misiaszek and Carlos Alberto Torres

This series of short-format books provide readers a diverse range of Paulo Freire's work and Freireans' reinventions toward social justice both inside and outside education, without readers needing any prior knowledge of his scholarship. The books offer new perspectives on the work of Freire's teaching, ideas, methods, and philosophies. Each book will introduce Freire's work so it is easily understood by a wider audience without overly simplifying the depth of his scholarship.

Advisory Board

Also Available in the Series

Freire and Environmentalism: Ecopedagogy, Greg William Misiaszek

Freire and Critical Theorists, Crystal Green

Freire and Children's Literature, Ernest Morrell and Jodene Morrell

Freire's Key Terms, edited by Teresa García Gómez

Freire and Feminism, edited by Eunice Macedo

Freire and Student Empowerment, edited by Michaela Ensweiler

Freire and Drama

'Marília', a Play
Anti-Oppression and Healing in the Arts

ROGÉRIO M. PINTO

BLOOMSBURY ACADEMIC
LONDON · NEW YORK · OXFORD · NEW DELHI · SYDNEY

BLOOMSBURY ACADEMIC
Bloomsbury Publishing Plc, 50 Bedford Square, London, WC1B 3DP, UK
Bloomsbury Publishing Inc, 1359 Broadway, New York, NY 10018, USA
Bloomsbury Publishing Ireland, 29 Earlsfort Terrace, Dublin 2, D02 AY28, Ireland

BLOOMSBURY, BLOOMSBURY ACADEMIC and the Diana logo are
trademarks of Bloomsbury Publishing Plc

First published in Great Britain 2026

Series design by Charlotte James
Cover image © Paulo Freire via Torres, Carlos Alberto (2014).
First Freire: Early writings in social justice education. Teachers
College Press. Background image © ilyast / Getty Images

Bloomsbury Publishing Plc does not have any control over, or responsibility
for, any third-party websites referred to or in this book. All internet
addresses given in this book were correct at the time of going to press.
The author and publisher regret any inconvenience caused if addresses
have changed or sites have ceased to exist, but can
accept no responsibility for any such changes.

A catalogue record for this book is available from the British Library.

A catalog record for this book is available from the Library of Congress.

ISBN: HB: 978-1-3504-7486-4
         PB: 978-1-3504-7487-1
       ePDF: 978-1-3504-7489-5
      eBook: 978-1-3504-7488-8

Series: Freire in Focus

Typeset by Integra Software Services Pvt. Ltd.
Printed and bound in Great Britain

For product safety related questions contact productsafety@bloomsbury.com.

To find out more about our authors and books visit www.bloomsbury.com
and sign up for our newsletters.

CONTENTS

FIGURES

SERIES EDITORS' FOREWORD: CONFRONTING THE EXILE OF OUR SOUL

Carlos Alberto Torres[1]

Distinguished Professor, Director, Paulo Freire Institute, University of California Los Angeles (UCLA)

This book by Professor Rogério Meireles Pinto is an exceptional literary and artistic product blending political analysis, education, art, and literature, all of it in the celebration of life while confronting oppression. But it is not only a model of denunciation but a call for transformation, with his unique way to blend art-based scholarly research with community engaged work. In his introduction he tells us with his uniquely pristine prose:

Autobiographical drama and performance as tools at the community level can help abate or neutralize the lies and

---

[1]Paris, September 10, 2025.

misinformation such as those I grew up with, peddled by Brazilian politicians and religious leaders during and even after the dictatorship. Today, this depraved behavior is on full display globally, with alliances between Trump of the United States, Vladimir Putin of Russia, Viktor Orbán of Hungary, Jair Bolsonaro of Brazil, and Nayib Bukele of El Salvador.

One of the powerful lessons of this book is that it is from our life experience, and lessons and learning acquired that our lifeworld can be comprehended. Like it or not, critical personal narratives, even at the risk of placing oneself and our voice as a genre, are counter narratives, testimonies, and stories that may disrupt, incommode, or upset people because they may be quite removed from what used to be the standard politeness of academic work.

This storytelling sociology is now having a more prominent role in the work of people concerned with speaking about social justice. More so when this book gives us also methods and tools for performing artistically with our students, or simply among our circle of friends. A soul-searching pedagogical practice that profoundly influences our own identity formation, a lifelong learning process.

But reading this book shall be done with special attention not only to the text but to the context in which the message is being played out in the United States and given the growing presence of a new authoritarianism, reverberating globally for the moment. Because of the conditions instituted under the Trump[2] administration, it is expected that the psychological crises that university professors will witness in their classes, among themselves and their students, will continue to deepen, and more events connected with burnout and depression, as well as feelings of despair, anxiety, hopelessness, and intense emotional distress in many segments of the population will be common sense expression of alienation of our daily lives and routines.

One of the many achievements that Professor Rogério Pinto crafted subtly in this formidable little book combining different revolutionary traditions of literature, art, and critical education is a robust sense of hope, one that reverberates in each of the sentences that claims suffering but, at the same time, reconciliation with oneself, with the nature that surround us, even with our dreams and commons sense, with our antinomies of the past, with our fears for the future. A reconciliation that it is not only subjective but collective.

It is this spirit of reconciliation between critique and celebration of life that allows Professor Pinto (or shall I say Marília?) to guide into a most profound exploration of our souls, dreams, fears, and wishes for hope to make this a better world. In the words of Freire in his masterful book *Pedagogy of the Oppressed*, a world in which it will be easier to love.

ACKNOWLEDGMENTS

This book is dedicated to the millions of children who die or become disabled every year due to preventable accidents.

I wish to thank my research assistants, Evan Hall, Sarya Shehadeh, and Vitalis Im, who did the preliminary review of the literature upon which I built the different chapters of this book. Their dedication to this project was inspiring and their work was detailed and accurate.

I thank David Pratt, my spouse, for his expert feedback on several portions of the original manuscript. His love and dedication to my pursuits inspire me every day. *Obrigado, meu amor.*

INTRODUCTION

Why use drama and performance for social and political liberation? What happens when audience members identify with the characters of plays that focus on the protagonist's life experiences and the sociopolitical and economic contexts that define their existences?

In *Freire and Drama—Marília: A Play*, I build on key concepts developed by Paulo Freire (*Pedagogy of the Oppressed*) and later reinvented by August Boal (*Theatre of the Oppressed*) to show the potential of drama and performance and other art forms to spark deep reflection and action toward social and political liberation ("liberation").

Liberation: In *Pedagogy of the Oppressed*, Freire (200C) contends that, through reflection *and* action, human beings can become free of the sociopolitical and economic forces used by the powerful to oppress and denigrate them. Freire believed that "The liberation of the oppressed is a liberation of women and men, not things"; and that, "Attempting to liberate the oppressed without their reflective participation in the act of liberation is to treat them as objects that must be saved from a burning building" (p. 101).

While I agree with the spirit in Freire's claim, "The liberation of the oppressed is a liberation of women and men, not things," I would like to move away from the binary "women and men," as gender is not the only form of identity that defines human beings. Both Freire and Boal have used the terms "man" to indicate human being(s), the corresponding of which in English would be "mankind." I wish to highlight this point to emphasize that Freire and Boal provided an essential initial push toward humanizing oppressed people by stating that people are not things, that they have dignity and self-determination, and ought not to be manipulated by the ruling classes.

More contemporary feminist approaches to understanding liberation not only use more inclusive language but also explicitly challenge patriarchy, a system that presupposes the "male" as the center of the family and society. Bárbara Santos's *Teatro das Oprimidas* (2023) offers concrete methods and techniques for understanding and practicing the teachings of Freire and Boal concerning the liberation of all human beings. Santos's book carries Boal's title, *Teatro do Oprimido*, but here she uses the gendered adjective "*oprimidas*" ("oppressed") instead of "*oprimido*." By making it plural and using the feminine adjective, Santos underscores the inclusion of women/females. Santos and other contemporary writers have been more inclusive of transgender people, something that was overlooked by both Freire and Boal. In her book, Santos explores the portrayal of myriad forms of oppression from an intersectional perspective that includes gender, race, class, sexual orientation, and other social identities.

Freire and Drama—Marília: A Play aims to show how Freire's theoretical concepts helped to create theatrical vehicles that would help me, and other individuals and communities, reflect critically on issues at the root of oppressive systems—healthcare, criminal justice, the government itself, etc. The use of personal narratives in live performances—referred to as self-referential theater—became popular in and around the globe, including in Brazil, in the 1970s, the decade during which Freire and Boal published *Pedagogy of the Oppressed* and *Theatre of the Oppressed,* respectively. Self-referential theater broadcasts the voices of the oppressed (Heddon, 2008). Personal experience used in performance follows from self-determination and liberatory action meant to decolonize public discourse and patriarchy. Resisting oppression can mean revealing its sociopolitical and economic sources, a strategy both Freire and Boal used in their lives and teachings. For me, self-referential theater means the performance of the lives and conflicts of real people. For example, the genesis and content of my one-person play, *Marília,* is based on the lives of real people, including my sister Marília, the raison d'être for the play, and my entire family. The text is about our lives and struggles, and the drama that unfolds in the performance of *Marília* represents my reason for wanting to embed a playscript in a scholarly work. By using self-referential drama and real people's conflict, I will show how to bring life and relevance to scholarly work concerning the roots and consequences of myriad forms of oppression.

From Boal's perspective, conflicts need not always be resolved by the end of the performance because the lives and conflicts of real people continue beyond the parameters of a performance (Dunne, 2016; Santos, 2016). Liberatory drama and performance carry social awareness, social justice, and advocacy agendas (Pinto, 2022a; Saldãna, 2003; Spry, 2010). Prime examples of socially engaged art have been internationally recognized. For example, *Die Dreigroschenoper* (*Threepenny Opera*, 1928, Bertolt Brecht, adapted from a translation by Elisabeth Hauptmann, music by Kurt Weill). This incredible work was adapted/reinvented as the Brazilian musical play *Ópera do Malandro* (*The Scoundrel's Opera*, Chico Buarque, 1979). Keith Haring's (1989) visual art "Silence = Death" became a symbol of AIDS activism and the struggles of the real person who was infected by the virus that eventually claimed his life. Another example is the work of Joan Baez, a singer, songwriter, musician, and activist whose career has been running from 1958 to the present. All these different works, to different degrees, stand for resistance, protest, and social justice. When I think of the power of drama that involves real people, I wish the readers of this book to think about the impact of these great works that will forever be imprinted in our collective consciousness.

Moreover, there are numerous contemporary works, using *Theatre of the Oppressed* theory and practices, discussed in later chapters, with which my autobiographical work presented here, my one-person play Marília, is in communication. For example, in celebration of the Day of Black Women, the theater group, *Coletivo Madalena Anastácia*, based in Rio de Janeiro, presented the play, *Qual é o seu Lugar?* (*What's Your Place?*; Director: Bárbara Santos) at the *Centro de Teatro do Oprimido* (Theater of the Oppressed Center), in Rio. By taking the form of a question, the title suggests the study of how Black women gained power and made socioeconomic strides over the past several decades while losing ground due to racist and sexist social and political dynamics. By asking poignant questions, the play represents an intervention whose aim is to change the social context around the questions the women ask, e.g., "What spaces do we wish to occupy?"; "What spaces do we need to build?" The show celebrates the success of the first ten years of the Teatro das Oprimidas and its fight against racism and sexism. For more details about this and other major contemporary plays, please visit the Centro Teatro do Oprimido at https://www.ctorio.org.br/home/

Another example of contemporary work with which my one-person play communicates, *Pactos para Reflorestar a Terra* (*Pacts to Reforest the Earth*; Directors: Desirée Santos and Renato Linhares), was produced by the Serviço Social do Comércio, Copacabana, Rio de Janeiro, in July 2025. This play invites the audience to imagine the future and the myriad natural disasters and social difficulties that will come about, specifically in the Maré, a neighborhood in Rio de Janeiro comprised of fifteen *favelas* alongside Guanabara Bay. Reflecting themes of loss, which also appear in my play, the *Pactos* characters, using LGBTQIA+ life experiences as a jumping-off point, seek different ways of surviving the deleterious effects of modernity and reimagine ways to *reforest* the earth. For more details, I suggest the Centro Teatro do Oprimido website (above).

Akin to the central goal of the socially engaged artworks mentioned above, the theatrical text herein, my one-person play *Marília*, aims to reveal conflicts set in motion by the oppression that I and my family experienced, and it poses questions to help audience members critically reflect on myriad forms of oppression. I invite the readers or audience members to engage in actual critical dialogues and reflection. Examples of potential audiences for this book include high school English or Theater/Drama students, university undergraduates and postgraduates in Education, Literature, Playwriting, Brazilian and Latinx Studies, Queer Studies, or other courses with Diversity, Equity, and Inclusion (DEI) content. This book may also appeal to theatergoers or *littérateurs* outside of academic settings who are interested in work employing an anti-oppression lens. I echo aspects of social movements (e.g., feminist, queer, and immigrant movements) that may act outside of formal learning spaces, hoping to engage readers, including advocates and activists, beyond traditional academia.

This book's central piece is the text of *Marília*, my solo play exploring the life of a poor family during the dictatorship in Brazil, the losses they faced, and the protagonist's decision to immigrate to the United States. *Marília* explores the protagonist's use of Freire's theoretical approaches, Boal's theatrical practices, and communicates with Santos's (2023) intersectional approach to make sense of his life as a gender nonconforming, queer, poor immigrant, who is today a full professor in a prestigious American university.

Liberation and Critical Consciousness

Freire's definition of liberation in *Pedagogy of the Oppressed* was as inclusive as it could have been in its era. Written in Portuguese, it was published in Portugal in 1972 and Brazil in 1974. Freire wrote as a citizen of Brazil, then suffering a brutal dictatorship, the result of a military coup that persecuted Freire and led to his exile, ultimately lasting until 1980. Though Freire sought to demonstrate the deleterious effects of the experience of living in a political and economic environment characterized by disparate social classes, poverty, and hunger in Brazilian society, his sentiments recur today in discourse and action around DEI efforts at the time of this writing under attack in the United States.

I was born the year after the 1964 military coup in Brazil. I learned of Freire and studied his methods at the Universidade Federal de Minas Gerais (1983–7; the dictatorship ended in 1985), where I studied biological sciences and education. Freire returned to Brazil in 1980 and was reinstated as a professor at the Federal University of Pernambuco in 1987. My interest in and work toward liberation was founded on my passion for the idea that all human beings deserve respect and a chance to flourish, regardless of who they are or in what conditions they are born. In my work, and my life, I celebrate *all* possible social identities that humans possess.

> **Flourishing:** Lynn Soots suggests that "Flourishing is the product of the pursuit and engagement of an authentic life that brings inner joy and happiness through meeting goals, being connected with life passions, and relishing in accomplishments through the peaks and valleys of life" (Soots, 2015).

Flourishing is a key goal for human beings (Soots, 2015). It has been described and measured in the positive psychology literature as a multidimensional concept, including extraversion, social support, well-being, happiness, life satisfaction, and physical and spiritual health. Though this book is not about flourishing, I bring it up in the context of Freire because the "flourishing" literature has, for almost two decades, advanced the concept of "conscientiousness" as a personality trait and state of well-being that facilitates "flourishing" (Huppert & So, 2011; Seligman, 2012).

"Conscientiousness" ("conscienciosidade" in Portuguese) differs from Freire's concept of *"conscientização"* (in Portuguese), often translated as "awareness." However, in this book, I use the term "critical consciousness," as it is most often used in the social science and education literature.

> **Critical Consciousness and Oppression:** Freire (2000) contended that human beings are fully equipped with intellectual and emotional capacities to comprehend the social, cultural, and political environment around them. Human beings are fully capable of taking personal and collective action against the oppression perpetrated against them—oppression being the method used by ruling classes to exploit by violence the labor of poor people, and to marginalize and minoritize groups of people based on its members' social identities. This method is in full display in the current Trump's administration, as myriad Executive Orders have been issued for the purpose of withholding social and public health services and educational opportunities humans deserve and need for self-realization and a flourishing society.

Positive psychology is concerned about individual-level development and flourishing, but Freire's work underscores the value and significance of education and critical consciousness as key ingredients for building a flourishing society. For Freire, education is a practice of freedom aimed at helping human beings develop self-awareness and wish to make society more equitable and inclusive. His writings suggest that teachers and governments should support flourishing across all sectors of society. Attempts across the globe to advance DEI have been the latest and perhaps most organized since the 1960s, as well as social movements in academia, government, and other private and public sectors. Current attacks on DEI suggest that the US government fears what DEI efforts have accomplished and what they can do going forward.

Drama and Performance Abate Oppression

I am troubled by how our ability to flourish can be hampered by socioeconomic and political pressure. Human beings often internalize their oppressors' lies and demands. The second Trump presidency demonstrates how internalization of the oppressor's message—elevating the elite and denigrating marginalized people who might benefit from DEI efforts—can lead to the choice of a leader known for his ability to perform hatred and disdain for those marginalized people. About 33 percent of the electorate did not vote in the 2024 presidential election, whose winner promised to behave like a dictator on his first day. About 31 percent cast votes for Trump, many having internalized his lies and misinformation about white cisgender Christian male superiority among others.

Autobiographical drama and performance as tools at the community level can help abate or neutralize the lies and misinformation such as those I grew up with, peddled by Brazilian politicians and religious leaders during and even after the dictatorship. Today, this depraved behavior is on full display globally, with alliances between Trump of the United States, Vladimir Putin of Russia, Viktor Orbán of Hungary, Jair Bolsonaro of Brazil, and Nayib Bukele of El Salvador.

Freire exposed the conditions under which Brazilians lived throughout my childhood, adolescence, and early adulthood. He also gave us a gift. He developed and taught methods now used globally to combat lies and misinformation that foster oppressed people's beliefs that there is something wrong with *them*. Those who internalize oppression often disengage themselves from civic and political activities, including voting, that could improve our lives and promote societal flourishing. We disengage ourselves to avoid psychological and existential pain stemming from oppression and hopelessness. We trade these for short-lived feelings of safety and comfort without realizing that our civic and political silence only empowers our oppressors. Among his twenty lessons in *Tyranny: Twenty Lessons from the the Twentieth Century*, Snyder (2017) alerts us not to obey in advance. I believe that obedience and silence equal colluding with the oppressor and it is antithetical to liberation.

I present *Marília*, my one-person play, to show how drama and performance can help people identify and critique the oppressor's negative messages. This understanding of the power of personal narrative and drama I owe to Freire's pupil August Boal. In 1971, Boal was identified as a threat to Brazil's military regime, and was arrested, tortured, and exiled to Argentina. During his five years in exile, Boal wrote and published *Theatre of the Oppressed*, outlining a type of theater that would enable performers and spectators to collaborate, acting out parts that provide solutions to social, political, and economic problems.

Interaction: In the Foreword of *Theatre of the Oppressed*, Boal asserted that "all must act, all must be protagonists in the necessary transformations of society." Boal contended that direct interactions between actors and audiences could improve communication among individuals with different oppressed social identities. These individuals share a common humanity. This connects to Freire's belief that human beings are not things.

My life growing up and how I came to the United States is the subject of *Marília*, which I wrote after my mother's death in 2012. I performed the play at the United Solo Festival on Theater Row in New York City in 2015 and again at the Vrystaat Arts Festival, Bloemfontein, South Africa, in 2016. Following Boal's basic tenets of the *Theatre of the Oppressed*, *Marília* started outside the theater, where I greeted my audiences and asked them to tie a ribbon around their wrist and make a wish. I used a black ribbon to create awareness about accidents, the leading cause of death among children, including that of my sister, Marília, who died when she was hit by a bus in front of the building where we grew up. The play was written not to incorporate every possible opportunity for interaction suggested by Boal but to evoke empathy among audience members who might share one or more of the oppressions that defined and still does define my existence.

Growing up, I felt close to my dead sister, as though she were alive inside me. We talked and played together. I pretended to be her by creating the voice I thought she might have had. I created her walk, thoughts, feelings, and mannerisms. I felt compelled to tell our story live on a stage, at a theater, or on a street corner. The play addresses Marília's death and my father's molestation of me and my older sisters (except Marília, who died too young). I grew up confused about my gender identity and I questioned whether or not I might be my family's "replacement" for my dead sister. The script incorporates many props, projections, music, and sound cues. I use songs and fragments of poetry to advance the plot while providing breaks from the narrative. The script establishes the cultural context of my family traumas by portraying points along my journey from poverty in Brazil to a life and career as a university professor in the United States—from early loss and gender confusion to family reconciliation and reconstitution.

I ask the audience to imagine themselves in my shoes and to reflect on their own lives and the oppressions to which they might have been subjected. I ask them to consider their social identities and positionalities and evaluate their roles, as oppressors and/or oppressed, in maintaining a prejudicial and unequal society. As a one-person show, *Marília* was never conceived as an example of forum theater, Boal's most known approach to *Theatre of the Oppressed*, in which many people are involved in creating the script. *Marília* allowed me to revisit my early life, including the moments that I internalized the oppressor's messages aimed to diminish me as something other than a human being and the moments I played the role of an oppressor by normalizing my privileges, for example, my light skin color. *Marília*'s script was crafted to evoke conversations between me and my audience and between the people who came to hear my story. For more details about how *Marília* came to be, I recommend a book chapter I wrote in 2022 that deals with autoethnographic playwriting and drama for self-healing and advocacy (Pinto, 2022b).

Freire and Boal

I live by the conviction that human beings deserve the basic necessities of life—nutritious food, affordable housing, and healthcare—simply because we are human beings. Growing up poor, the youngest of eight siblings, during the Brazilian dictatorship, my family's basic needs were never fully met. We lived in a small two-bedroom apartment in one of the nine buildings on a housing project. It was hot in the summer and cold in the winter. Public utilities, such as water and electricity, were very expensive and therefore unstable at best. The ten of us shared one bathroom. Food, also expensive, particularly any form of protein, was never sufficient. I was hungry, but I developed the capacity to function without enough food by faking that I did not like different types of basic foods like beans and/or that I was not hungry. My father died at the age of forty-three for lack of medical care.

As humanists, Freire and Boal affirmed that no one should grow up like this. They said that all of us have the potential to overcome these obstacles, but they also contended that we all need structural changes to help us flourish. We become more human by developing the capacity to feel empathy for one another, which in turn creates a sense of well-being. Freire and Boal believed that the oppressor and the oppressed were stripped of their humanity. Freire and Boal developed the basis for a global literature demonstrating the techniques via which oppressors and oppressed can better determine the extent of their powers and vulnerabilities. Based on their life experiences, they aimed to teach and inspire us to develop new methods and to reinvent their practices in order to achieve liberation no matter what the current sociopolitical and economic environment might be. Therefore, I "reinvent" Freire's concepts in this book by using Boal's inspiration and techniques, but from an intersectional approach unearthed by Bárbara Santos and other contemporary writers. I will show how autobiographical content in the form of drama and performance can inspire oppressed people to engage in reflection and action toward liberation. I will also show how specific dramatic contents can affect positive health and well-being.

This book covers subject matters concerning oppression and several root causes by using colloquial and dramatic writing.

In Part I, I present *Marília,* my own one-person play about my family living under social, political, and economic conditions still widespread across the globe. The play runs 75 minutes, contains ten sub-sections ("monologues"), and two poems that can be used separately or together for deep discussions and for students and actors to practice monologue delivery. Inspired by Freire's use of critical questions to spark community conversations and reflection, *Marília* focuses on a set of oppressive conditions and prejudices to be highlighted in Part II.

In Part II, Chapter 1, "Oppression and Prejudice Depicted in Biographical Drama and Performance," I will show that xenophobia, racism, homophobia, transphobia, and poverty can contribute to overall oppression and internalization of oppressive messages. Here, I use passages from *Marília,* alongside photographs, to demonstrate the usefulness of dramatic text and performance in shedding light on and promoting critical reflections around these issues. In Chapter 2, "Arts-Based Methods for Critical Dialogues and Liberation," I describe how Freire's and Boal's theories and anti-oppression methods are interconnected and how we can use them to promote liberation by using drama and performance, whatever the sociopolitical and economic environment might be. In Chapter 3, "Biographical Drama and Performance for Self-Healing and Liberation," I show the usefulness of drama and performance, with special emphasis on solo performance, as essential tools for sparking critical dialogues, reflection, action, self-healing, and advocacy. In Chapter 4, "Drama and Performance to Cultivate Empathy and Well-Being," I present and discuss theoretical and empirical evidence showing how different art practices, with special emphasis on drama and performance, have been used successfully to help reduce oppression by improving human being's empathy for one another and their own well-being.

In the Conclusion, I summarize the book and provide concluding thoughts aimed at setting the next steps for further exploration of drama and performance as liberation tools.

In the Appendix, I provide instructions for two workshops, based on my one-person play *Marília*, that can be used among groups of readers and/or viewers of *Marília* to inspire reflection and action.

This book is not all-inclusive. It is an introduction to how Freire's educational theories and Boal's *Theatre of the Oppressed* together demonstrate the usefulness of drama and biographical narratives to spark critical dialogues and critical reflection around issues created by oppressive forces: xenophobia, racism, homophobia, transphobia, and poverty. Using an intersectional lens, I present how these myriad forms of oppression influence how human beings deal with death, grief and loss, gender non-conformity, sexual orientation, and immigration status. Herein, I provide a vision of how autobiographical material can support critical dialogues about global political affairs, especially conditions that resemble the Brazilian dictatorship of 1964–85. I hope the innovative nature of this book, which contains the text of a play that has been performed several times, will engage those involved in the arts and social sciences, particularly social work. I hope it will engage theater-makers and theatergoers in the process of research and scholarship building, and pedagogical practices to improve understanding of connections between art and social justice. This will support contemporary discourses around DEI and threats to it and serve as a springboard for cutting-edge artistic research and practice to address contemporary issues such as racism, xenophobia, and colorism, and move us toward liberation.

FIGURE 0 Marília
Scanned photo (Circa 1966) by Rogério M. Pinto. From family archive
of vintage photos depicting Marília at the age of about two and half.

PART ONE

Freire and Drama
Marília: A Play

MARÍLIA: A PLAY

CAST OF CHARACTERS

Protagonist: Rogério ("R"), gay male, grew up poor in Brazil, currently a university professor.

Marília: Protagonist's 3-year-old, youngest sister = Life size doll

Additional characters played by the protagonist:

Cida: R's mother

Suzana: R's oldest sister

Patricia: R's second oldest sister

Millie: R's third oldest sister

Context: Ash Wednesday, the day after carnaval. The stage is R's home. R has travelled for the past 24 hours from Brazil to NYC and just arrived home. R greets the audience as they enter the theater.

Setting: Each program has a Black Ribbon (Meaning: accident and childhood injury prevention) *that says, "Marília."* The ribbon should be narrow and long enough to go around the wrist.

Stage: Surface *for projections and large suitcase. Inside suitcase: life size doll of Marília* covered with a veil *and two boxes. Small box: Marília's remains. Medium-size box: candies, cookies and props for R's mother and sisters.*

Projections and music: All projections can be requested or they can be replaced based on the person performing the monologue. The author recommends the use of images that will mostly speak to the audiences intended to experience the play. The same is true about the music used in some of the scenes.

Arrival

This is fabulous! [*Surveys audience*] I'm so excited to see you! So glad you came to hear the story of Marília. Thank you so much for coming, it means a lot to me.

Wow! So many trips ... I just came back from Brazil, where I was born, where I grew up and lived before I came here, in 1987. [*Heavy pause*]

I'm exhausted from traveling, carrying heavy suitcases. I've been travelling for the past 24 hours. It's a long way from Brazil. [*Projection #1: Brazil-USA directions*]

Yesterday, I left my mother's place at noon to catch the 3 PM shuttle from Belo Horizonte my hometown to Rio de Janeiro. It took less than one hour, but in Rio I waited for seven hours before departing to New York. We took off on time at 11 PM and flew for nine hours. It is a long trip!

[*Projection #1 fades*]

But I love each visit to Brazil. Belo Horizonte has grown so much with a population of three million, and Rio de Janeiro more than six million. Belo and Rio are among the nicest cities in Latin America; and yet I came to live here in New York City ... I love the city even after 28 years! But to this day, I still adore the richness of Brazil's history, culture and folklore.

[*Carnaval Music: "Cidade Maravilhosa" by A. Filho in "O Maior Carnaval do Mundo" cut #1*]

This trip included four days of carnaval! It was sunny! It was summer! It was *fabulous*! Since I was a child, Carnaval is my favorite holiday. People, all over, playing wonderful music, dancing, wearing stunning costumes like the beautiful woman I saw yesterday on my way to the airport. [*Projection #2: Woman with headdress*] Every year, life in Brazil takes a four-day halt and people, old and young, Black and white, male and female all embrace beauty, desire, fantasy, and hope for better days to come. Carnaval is a "welcome" to all, it stretches social boundaries that outside carnaval would be a real drag!

[*Projection #3: Protagonist in drag*]

   [*Dances and poses*]
   [*Projection #3 fades*]
   Yesterday was the last day of carnaval.
   [*Carnaval Music Fades*]

In Rio, I contemplated the Christ on the Hill, [*Projection #4: Christ the Redeemer*] His welcoming arms inviting us to stop, pray, listen ... Today, Ash Wednesday; we look upon the Christ and from the ashes we bear His cross, a reminder of our mortality. [*Crosses forehead*]

[*Projection #4 fades*]

Lent is here: forty days of fasting and abstinence. But fasting in Brazil is hard to do! Brazilian food is absolutely delicious; a mix of indigenous, African and Portuguese cuisines .... Just to name a few! When I'm there, I eat way too much—pounds of candies, delicious candies! I gain ten pounds in my belly and come back looking pregnant. [*Caresses belly*].

Do I look pregnant to you?

I love to bring souvenirs from Brazil; little things that have meaning to me. Like the black ribbon I got for you. [*Takes ribbon out of pocket*] In Brazil, they say that if you have a special wish, you should tie a ribbon, like this, around your wrist, and ask God to grant you that wish. If you have faith, your wish will be granted when the ribbon gets old and breaks loose. Please try it! But make sure to make a special wish. Like the one I've had for the longest time. For so long, I've wanted to tell the story of Marília. I'm glad you came to hear it.

*

Marília was the youngest of my five sisters ... I also have two brothers. I'm the youngest of eight siblings, I'm the baby! I love all my brothers and sisters and someday I might tell each of their life stories.

But today I will tell you about Marília. I was 10 months old when she died. Marília was three years old. It's strange, as an adult, to think of my elder baby sister who died on the last day of carnaval (the day we call Fat Tuesday in the United States). It was summer, February, 1966. Yesterday, the last day of carnaval was the anniversary of her death.

My mother tells me that the day Marília died, Marília took my mother's lipstick and smeared it all over her lips; did the same to me and to our little pet rabbit! With Marília's encouragement, I kept pulling the rabbit by the tail over and over until it made funny faces. Marília, very worried, rushes to tell my mother, Mommy, mommy, o *Rogerinho 'ta matando seu gatinho*—Little Rogério is killing your little cat! [*Pause*]

I don't remember any of it; I wasn't even one year old.

My mother tells me that, later that day, Marília died; she was in a fatal accident involving the local bus that stopped in front of our building. I often asked my mother to tell me more about it, but she would say that that was all I needed to know; that and that Marília looked like an angel in her casket.

I grew up conjuring up all sorts of images about a little angel in a white box inside the earth. I was curious about how the long wings could fit inside the little box.

But I knew not to ask. [*Pause*]
[*Unpacks medium-size box*]

Discoveries

Every time I unpack, I can't help but think about when I left Brazil to come to the United States, March 24, 1987, right after college.

I took four years of biological sciences. College for me was in Belo Horizonte; I lived at home. I attended classes all day and worked as a teacher's assistant. I loved anything to do with biology! But growing up I also had a dream to become a hairdresser! I was good at hairdressing!

Over the years, I had cut and styled my mother's hair and all my sisters', except Marília's ... but I wondered ... what type of hair might she have? [*Pause*] How did she look like? You see, my only reference was a faded photography on her grave. Like I said, I was good at hairdressing! I went to college *and* beauty school in Brazil. Everyone was surprised! Eventually everyone celebrated my decision! Hairdressing even helped me to stay in the United States. I worked for many years doing hair before I became a social worker and later on a university professor. But I'm getting ahead of myself here. Back to hairdressing! I went to beauty school in the evening. The school in Belo Horizonte was called Broadway! Imagine that! I think that my dream of becoming a hairdresser had something to do with my gender identity and how I expressed myself since I was a child.

As a little child I felt that my boy's body was quickly inhabited by my sister Marília ... please don't worry, I am not crazy nor did I ever have multiple personalities ... Though she was dead, Marília and I developed very close together; she made me stronger, capable to do a lot, but not without conflict!

I remember my mother asking the doctor "why is my son so much like his sister, why all his friends are girls, why is he feisty and yet so sensitive, is he normal, my son?" My mother's preoccupations haunted me all my life and made me fearful about my future.

In college, I was under the impression that I could never be a successful biologist because I wasn't "manly" enough. I could never be a successful biologist because I wasn't "feminine" enough. I had better grades than most students, but Brazil had been under a dictatorship since the 1960s; in the 1980s, when I was in college, there was no LGBT liberation yet. No transgender liberation in sight! Being feminine and having a boy's body, I feared I'd be beat up and killed by bigots and the military police. The discrimination I'd have to overcome as a biologist seemed (it was) insurmountable. There were voices from my childhood echoing inside my head over and over and over.

[*Emotionally distressed*]
Bichinha! *Mulherzinha*! *Veado*!
Sissy! Little girl! Faggot! These voices were meant to drown me.

The same straight boys who mocked me also chased me around as though I was a girl. In public, they taunted me; in private, in a twisted way, they seduced me into doing things for them, sexual things. I was confused by all this. Even more confused when adults asked me, "Are you a boy or a girl?" I was asked often, "Are you a boy or a girl," even after I became a teenager.

As a child, I thought what made a girl a girl was having a pussy. All my sisters had pussies. If I had one, I'd be just like Marília, right? A Marília who never died. In my mind, everyone thought I might be a girl. I knew I was a girl, even though I didn't have a pussy. I began to wonder if my father also knew I was a girl … the way he looked at me … showed special interest in me … I was confused … you see, my father touched me intimately. His touch was firm, manly; he was a man. Therefore, I must be a "girl." [*Pause*] Perhaps Marília? My father was so sad after she died … May be if I was Marília, could I make him happy again!?

I guess I'll never know. Marília was gone for seven years when my father died. By then, I was eight years old. It must've been hard for him to make sense of his behaviors. I think he felt overwhelmed with guilt and died at the age of forty-three. I saw him in the hospital in a lot of pain. His cancer took over both his lungs.

[*Projection # 5: Father's photo*]

Oh! My father …
He must've been lonely, my father
A life of losses and secrets
A wife and kids

What did he hope for, my father?
To have another daughter
Someone to love him
To touch the girl who died so young

I'm here, daddy … please don't make me wait

He must've been horny, my father
A life of losses and secrets
A wife and kids

What could he hope for, my father?
His son willing to obey
Someone to adore him
To lock the bedroom door and acquiesce

I'm here, daddy … please don't make me wait

He liked when the boy touched his feet
The warmth he felt in his gut
The tender touch of little fingers
The rise and fall of his penis
A sense of defeat

Was it all that my father desired?

If he wanted love,
Had I known he was about to die and decay,
I'd give him love …
All I wanted was for my daddy to stay

[*Projection # 5 fades*]

[*More unpacking to Carnaval Music*]
[*Carnaval Music: "As Pastorinhas" by João de Barro—Noel Rosa in "O Maior Carnaval do Mundo" cut #8*]

Brain

Yesterday, I spent a few hours with Clara, my old college professor. Overtime we have become really good friends. Clara came to the airport in Rio to keep me company until my departure. The airport was quiet, except for those of us trying to leave carnaval behind.

[*Carnaval Music Fades*]

Clara was a fabulous teacher and mentor. I was her assistant for three years. She was tough and detailed, and I adored her! Together we taught *Human Histology*—the intricacies and beauty of human tissues that make up all our organs.

I was fascinated by the human brain, [*Projection #6: brain*] how it works, how we feel and do things. The brain is soft, it must be protected against everything, [*Pause*] including awful accidents. Thick layers of bone [*Projection #7: brain inside the skull*] and connective tissues protect the brain against intrusion and destruction. Without the brain there is no life, nothing! The brain controls everything we do and everything we feel. Brain cells [*Projection #8: slide of brain cells*] allow us to *feel* love, pleasure, pain … These miraculous cells are no less than the caretakers and the wardens of all our feelings and all our memories.

[*Projection #8 fades*]

Clara and I reminisced about my college years, how we became friends, how in spite of so many losses and lack of resources, I was the first in my family to graduate from a university. Clara was so proud that I had been class valedictorian … [*Projection #9: Behind podium*].

In my graduation speech, I said, [*Projection #10: On the mic*]

"I would like to thank my classmates and friends, all my teachers, and particularly my mother, sitting in the audience. Thank you all for these wonderful four year, for providing this graduating class the support we needed to learn and to build a life filled with wonder and realization."

[*Projection #10 fades*]

Transitions

But deep down, I needed more. I was ever so uncomfortable inside my own skin. I had many questions about who I was and how my dead sister figured in my life ... I needed some distance from my family and all I had known.

I finished college, borrowed money, and took off to New York City! I had a dream to fulfill: to become a hairdresser!

My arrival in New York was not smooth, oh no! My first home, the basement of a house got flooded as soon as I moved in; *flooded*, the entire basement became a pool of water! Thank God for a friend of a friend who helped me find an apartment in Woodside, Queens, where I lived for the next several months.

Guess what? That building's elevator caught fire; the entire apartment, the entire building was engulfed in smoke.

But there is more ... I couldn't get a hairdressing job, I didn't speak English. I didn't have a cosmetology license or a green card. I had no money and no job in sight ... Eventually I got a job as a dishwasher in a restaurant. I worked seven days a week for about $200 ... After that, I delivered pizza: believe it or not, I fell from the bike ... My next job was in construction; imagine that! Surprisingly, I did well putting up drywall, painting ... you know, butch stuff.

But it didn't last long ... one of the guys on that site attacked me. I was having lunch. He appeared out of nowhere. Like the bullies from my childhood, he called me names and then spread patching compound all over my face. I couldn't see a thing! The construction workers on the site helped me get out and wash my face, but I never went back there. I was scared!

Scared, but not alone ... Marília was there with me as she is with me always ... reminding me that when I came to New York, I was happy to have any job, even those so hard to do. Immigrants from poor countries come here under difficult conditions: terrible debts; some swim across dangerous waters and others may die of heatstroke or suffocation in shipping containers. [*Pause*] After all that, we'll happily do any job we can get, no matter where we come from.

I came from a housing project in Belo Horizonte. [*Projection #11: Housing Project*] There we played bare foot on the dirt, grass, and unpaved streets [*Projection #12: Project grounds*]. A long avenue connected the nine buildings to the center of the city—20 minutes by bus! We lived on the first floor of building number Four. Marília's accident took place at the bus stop in front of that building. [*Projection grounds# 12 fades*] From the building's open courtyard, we could see inside each apartment. We knew one another's intimate business. The police often raided the buildings without any apparent reason. Growing up under the dictatorship, lack of privacy was common place.

Ten of us lived in a tiny two-bedroom apartment, me, my mother and father, my brothers and sisters, and the little pet rabbit. I slept in the same bed with my two younger sisters, Gladys and Millie.

I asked them about Marília all the time. They told me that Marília was in a terrible accident. If I wanted to know more, I should ask my mother and my older sisters. The less I knew the more I fantasized about the little angel and her wings inside the white box ... [*Pause*] I was scared of the unknown ...

When my father died, I slept in my mother's bed, the only place I felt safe ... her voice was so soothing when she sang lullabies. [*Sings*]

"*Dorme nenê ... mamãe tem o que fazer ...*
tem roupa pra lavar e costura pra cozer ... "

Mother

My mother worked hard to feed us and yet she found the time to sing all the time ... Every day, she took two buses and walked up a hill for 30 minutes to get to the school where she worked as janitor and cook. Many a time I walked up that hill with her ... She cooked and scrubbed all day, then she came back home to cook dinner, do the laundry (by hand), and care for us, her own kids. My mother is truly fabulous! [*Projection # 13: Bull's painting*]

She is not a bull, but she has been like one: big; beautiful; grounded; loyal; and tender. She painted this bull for me. I think of it as her self-portrait. I cannot tell you how much I adore it! She signed this painting as "*Cida*," C-I-D-A, "*Cida*," but her full name is *A-pa-re-cida de Jesús*, "Apparition of Jesus." [*Projection # 14: Christ Redeemer. Words "Apparition of Jesus" across*] Our last name, *Pinto*, in Brazilian Portuguese, means "little chicken." Therefore, my mother's full name is "Apparition of Jesus Little Chicken!"

[*Projection 14 fades*]

Do you know what I call my mother? I call her Blondie, "Loura," [*Projection 15: Mother's face with the word "Loura" across*] because she has beautiful light hair, she is fierce, and looks awesome!

Though mostly nice and good, my mother can be terribly obtuse and even cruel sometimes. [*Projection#15 fades*] For instance, when my sister Gladys was getting married; I must've been about fifteen at that time ... I let my hair grow a bit longer so that I could get a new style for the wedding. Oh God! My long hair looked beautiful! As the hairdresser blew my hair with the big round brush, a miracle was taking place before my very eyes. My hair was straight! Was I happy that day? Feeling so good about how I looked ... Growing up, I had learned that straight hair was good and curly hair (like mine) was bad. You had either good or bad hair, and mine was bad! Having bad hair meant that I was unattractive, ugly, doomed! I felt that my *straight* hair could save my life! I couldn't wait to show my mother. But that day, she came home particularly exhausted and irritable ... when she saw "the hair that could save my life," she was not happy at all; she was furious, "Ficou parecendo uma puta!" My new hair made me look like a whore, she said! Some part of me enjoyed what she said ... (Talking about confusion ...) she imagined me as a woman, and a sexy one for that matter! But my mother's anger was so unexpected; she threatened to cut my hair real short when I slept. My mother is not a threatening person, but that day I was afraid of her. She called *me* a whore! So often I felt like one, from the moment my father touched me. I ended up getting a haircut I knew would appease my mother.

However, a few days later, I told her, "*Nunca mais a senhora ou qualquer pessoa vai decidir qualquer coisa a respeito do my cabelo, meu genero or como eu deva viver a minha vida!*" Never again will you or anyone else decide anything about my looks, my gender or how I should live my life! But that was not me alone … Marília and I would have a life free of gender constraints.

As you already know, a few years later, I came to New York and became a hairdresser.

"America"

After my initial job adventures, I looked for work in the *Daily News*. I found an ad that said*: "Looking for easy going hairdresser, comfortable cutting hair of both men and women."* I could easily manage this, but the ad also said: "*Hairdresser should have a cosmetology license and be fluent in English.*" After only five months in New York, this, I definitely could not manage! But I called the place anyway and made an appointment for an interview. This was a "Marília" moment, when she enables me to do things I could never do on my own. I was nervous; my English was good enough to survive but not to understand details and clients' preferences about their hair. You know how people can be so picky about their hair! [*Pause*] In my interview, I was polite and answered truthfully each question … but I did not disclose that my visa to stay in the United States was about to expire. When I went for my job interview, I was about to become an "illegal alien" … [*Projection #16: R's face, a caricature of an alien*] a threat to the United States of America! I was fearful that I could be deported.

[*Projection #16 fades*]

Much to my relief and surprise, Sonia, the beauty salon's owner, gave me a job on the spot and soon after, she began to work on my immigration papers.

The Department of Labor took two years to process my application. After that, it took five years for me to receive my green card, and another five to become an American citizen. By the time I received my green card, my dream of becoming a hairdresser was realized and my work at Sonia's beauty salon was complete. By then I had another dream to fulfill, to become a social worker.

In the 1990s, I did volunteer work helping patients with HIV and AIDS. This work quickly compelled me to become a professional social worker. My undergraduate degree in biology was easily validated in the United States. In two years' time, I earned a Master's degree in social work from Yeshiva University. They had a fabulous program for people with full-time jobs. We took classes in the evening and on Sundays. I was thirty-two when I finished the Master's program. I practiced social work for several years while I went to Columbia University for my PhD. Many years have passed ... Now I am a researcher and professor of social work in the University of Michigan ... I still do hair, here and there ... only David's really, my husband of 28 years. I enjoy doing his hair! So much has changed in my life and I sincerely hope there is still a lot more to come!

Baggage

Yesterday at the airport, the airline weighed my suitcases. I weighed my emotional baggage. It's hard coming back, no matter how many years have passed ... The check-in agent asked me to redistribute the contents of my suitcases to even out the weight. I did. [*Picks up a jar*] I picked up this jar of *tempeiro,* the food seasoning my mother made for me. Everyone could smell garlic even though the jar was tightly sealed … My mother made it for me. Of course, I could make it for myself. [*Jar down*] This has been true all my life; my mother and sisters have done things for me, given me so much I could never list it all …

[*Open & holds lipstick*]

Pink lipstick, light and delicate like Marília … [*Picks up mirror. Holds mirrors until the end of scene*] … a little mirror reflecting both our faces … little things that make us both happy. Without my mother and all my sisters, I would not be here today. I am at once each and all of them. [*Looking in the mirror as mother and sisters*] We protected *you*; we fed *you*; we took good care of *you*.

I feel so heavy … heavy and old … old and fat! Do I look fat? [*Puts mirror and lipstick down*] Growing up I was so skinny, a scrawny kid! There was never enough food. My mother and siblings worked hard all day to feed all of us … Alone all day, I would open the refrigerator hoping to find food I knew wasn't there, adjusting to the fact that the refrigerator was empty, the house was empty. I would close the refrigerator and feel utterly disappointed even though I already knew there was nothing there. I always hoped I'd find candies … lots of candies! Alone all day, I dreamed of dressing up as an angel and going to church for the coronation of the Virgin Mary. [*Projection 17: Mary's Coronation*]. Every year, every evening in May, the girls from the housing project came to church wearing flowing tunics and beautiful feather wings ready for the coronation pageant. From the church floor, I watched them go up on the altar; little angels flowing around singing at church. [*Projection 18: Coronation*] I knew all the songs; I sang along:

"*Mês de maio, mês de alegria …*

Cantemos louvores a Virgem Maria ...."

[*Projection #18 fades*]

After the pageant, the angels received little bags filled with candies. But only girls were allowed; and, according to the authorities, I was not a real girl. [*Picking up each type of sweets*] Alone all day, I dreamed of lollipops, chocolate candies, jelly beans, cookies, cookies, cookies, [*Scoops up candies from box*] all the sweet things the little angels got ... [*Throws candies in the air*] There they are, all the candies we could never have! I wasn't a real girl; Marília was dead! I've tried really hard to let go of my memories of loneliness and the hunger I felt in my belly, but those pesky brain cells I learned about in college won't let me forget a thing. My memories make me feel cold ...

So very cold ... [*Projection #19: NYC buried in snow*] As I felt the winter I came to New York ... [*Projection #20: NYC and falling snow*] One evening, coming home from the beauty salon, I felt profoundly alone, more than I had ever been, the only soul in a frozen city. The streets were empty; the freezing weather scared me. I missed my mother desperately; I was desperate for some warmth.

[*Projection #20 fades*]

The pace of the city and the cold weather pushed me to eat more, dare more, try new things. I even considered becoming a whore; some immigrants do. We look for warmth in strangers who may help us with money, sometimes food. I didn't have it in me to become a whore, but I wonder ... if I had a pussy and long straight hair ... if I looked like the beautiful woman I saw yesterday on my way to the airport, would I have? [*Pause*]

A few days ago, back in Brazil, I was talking with my mother about how I felt when I first came to New York and how I still hate that memory of the cold and the fierce loneliness I felt ... I don't know how, but I ended up revealing to her how I have imagined Marília in her coffin all these years—an angel, cold and lonely, deep in the earth. [*Pause*] What I said prompted my mother to show me a letter she had received from the public cemetery where Marília had been buried.

Fragments

The letter explained that heavy rains had shifted the ground and washed away all the children's graves; the city had plans to eliminate the children's section of the cemetery. We were legally compelled to unbury Marília and move her remains to another grave. My mother told no one else about this and waited for me to get to Brazil to help her resolve this matter. Of course I agreed to do it. Without fully realizing all that would be involved, I called the number listed in the letter and made an appointment for the procedures. Two days later, my mother and I were sitting in a cab on our way to the cemetery. We talked about everything, except what we were about to do. We talked about her painting classes, my niece's wedding and marriage equality. My mother explained that she didn't understand all the ramifications of this historic opportunity for LGBT people to get married, but she was happy that now I could do it. She surprised me when she said that, when I was growing up, her biggest fear was that I'd be alone without a companion ... she said she was happy that I had found David and how much she loves him. [*Pause*] The things my mother says, who would've thought ... I planted a kiss on her cheek right before we got out of the cab. The gravedigger and the police officer were waiting for us. They finished the paperwork and silently guided us to what remained of Marília's grave. [*Projection #21: Grave*]

[*Picks up box with fragments*]

There, the gravedigger swung his pick; the pick hit the ground; the ground opened. There we were inside the Brazilian earth.

[*Projection #21 fades*]

The pick pierced the ground over and over; the first few moments felt like an eternity waiting to see Marília, the angel in the box. [*Opens box and picks Marília's fragments inside*] Suddenly, from down below, I heard the muffled sound of metal against metal. The pick hit the handle of her coffin. [*Holding up the rusty handle*] I looked at my mother; she looked back "Is this the handle of her coffin?" I heard not a sound from her. Dirt piled around us. I began to dig with my bare hands, searching for anything I could find. Deep in the pile, I found pieces of fabric. [*Holding stained fabric*] Could this be from the dress she was wearing? I ask my mother; she nodded "yes." I kept searching … [*Holding stained white sock*] Deeper in the pile, I found her little sock, and deeper still, [*Holding small bones*] I found what appeared to be bones. "Look Loura, these must be her bones; Marília's little bones." And then, as if by a miracle, [*Holding lock of hair*] I found a lock of her hair … [*Holding another lock of hair*] and then another. Oh God! My baby sister's hair, so pretty, [*Caresses face with hair*] so soft, good hair! Loura, there is nothing here. No flesh! There is no more Marília. Oh Loura, I'm so sorry, so very sorry, my love. [*Projection #22: Mother sees remains*] Witnessing my mother's dismay, I asked the gravedigger, "where is my sister"? [*Pause*] [*Puts remains back in the box*]

Marília was not embalmed. Her socks and the lining of her coffin, being made out of nylon, were the only things the gravedigger expected to find, nothing else. [*Projection #22 fades*] [*Pause*]. Marília was exposed to the wet Brazilian earth for more than thirty years.

Her epitaph said: "*Fui para Deus e voltarei na memória de meus pais e meus irmãos.*" "I went to God and will be back for my parents and siblings." We've been waiting for her; but, after she died, all we had was the photograph attached to her grave. And now, what?

[Puts box with remains back in the suitcase]

She promised to go to God and come back to us. I waited but she never came. I brought her back.

[Unveils life size doll of Marília] Have you seen her? I cling to her; she clings back. Can you see her? *[Picks up Marília]* I cling to her; she clings back. Marília, my dead sister, lives on inside me.

[Dances with Marília to carnaval music]

[Carnaval Music "A Jardineira" by B. Lacerda—H. Porto in "O Maior Carnaval do Mundo" cut #2]

Accident

Do you like dancing like this? Mother says she used to play with you like this; she tells me you loved it. Did you?

[Carnaval Music Fades]

I try to remember things, but all I know is what they tell me, our mother and sisters—and that is not a lot! What do you know? I can hear your voice in my head: go on, talk to me. I've longed for you all my life, forever wanting to be with you, to be you: the girl angel I never was. Deep down, I thought that I'd see you intact in your coffin, untouched by men, free of obsession, inside the earth as if nothing ever happened. I desperately wanted to finally find *myself* looking pretty like you, but what did I find? Nothing! Bits and pieces! Who are you, little sister, lovely images or rotten fragments? I am so angry that no one was there to save you from that fucking bus. Where was everybody? Where?

[*R transforms into Cida, Marília's mother*]

Often I pretended to be your mother.

[*Picks up white handkerchief and sits*] I am your mother ...
[*Cleans Marília's face*] In my fantasy, I'd catch you and save
you right before the bus ... I'd sing lullabies to put you to sleep
and again in the morning to wake you up ...

> [*Cida sings*]
> "*Era o começo de um dia. Oh! Oh! Oh! Oh!*
> *Uma criança chorava, uma vida sumia*
> *Aquele olhar de ternura ... e a inocência das fábulas*
> *Oh! Marília! Eu não posso esquecer Oh! Marília*
> *Oh! Marília*"

I love the sound of my kids and to sing for them, for you my
baby; the song you liked so much! My baby daughter; I'm so
happy Rogério brought you back. Ever since you left; like him,
I also wished that I could be with you, but your brothers and
sisters needed me, so I stayed.

Rogério grew up to be your age ... by the age of three, he
sounded just like you, smelled just like you. Remember Didi,
his godmother? Sometimes she dressed him up in your clothes.
It was hard to tell the two of you apart. I was embarrassed
that my boy was so much like a girl and ashamed of myself for
wanting him to be just like you. Since he was a child, Rogério
has been asking me what happened to you, "Please mommy;
tell me more about Marília."

[Soft *Carnaval Music: "Tristeza"* by H. Lobo—Miltinho in
"*O Maior Carnaval do Mundo*" cut #6]

[*Cida to audience*] After we unburied my daughter, I finally
told Rogério. From the cemetery, we could hear the music ... It
felt like carnaval, 1966 ... [*Turns to look at projections*]

[Projection #23: Carnaval Scene]
[Projection #24: Street and housing project building]
[Projection #25: View of street and project building from inside the bus]
[Projection #26: Moving bus]
[Projection #27: Moving bus tire]
[Projection #28: The human brain]
[Projection #29: Bloody pavement]
[Projection #30: Human brain inside the split skull]
[Projection #31: Bloody pavement]
[Screams frantically]
Marília! Marília! Marília!
[Turns to audience; Marília's brain fall to the floor]
[Carnaval Music Fades]
[Projection #31 fades]
[Cida places Marília on suitcase rack and covers her body]

After all these years, I'm still asking myself if my daughter saw the tires before she closed her eyes.

Did she feel the weight of the bus? Did she even close her eyes? Did she see death coming? Did Marília feel any pain? I don't know what my daughter felt. Does anyone?

All I know is that early in the day Marília died, she smeared lipstick all over herself, Rogério and the pet rabbit. I asked my older daughters to clean them up and watch them while I went downtown to run some errands. I took my daughter Millie with me. But, before I left, I promised Marília that I'd bring cookies for her. She loved cookies! I came back a couple of hours later: Marília saw me on the bus and ran outside to greet me. She crossed in front of the bus. The driver didn't see her! Suddenly, there she was, my daughter lying on the pavement. I picked her up, carried her inside, placed her on the table and wrapped her. We buried her the next day. My baby looked like an angel.

This is all I can remember, but Suzana, my oldest daughter, should know more, she was supposed to watch Marília.

[Cida sits and becomes Suzana]

Sisters

[Cida sits and becomes Suzana]

My mother is right; I was supposed to watch Marília. [*Pause*] My guilt weighs heavily on me; but then now and again I ask myself, was she better off dead? [*Pause*] How long would've been before my father touched her? He touched Rogério, he touched me too, and Patricia, and Millie … he molested all of us.

The day Marília died, my father was working. No one called him; we didn't have a phone. I remember him crying, the poor man, he was so sad … After the wake, I watched him cutting a loaf of bread, one slice for him, one for my mother, and one for each of us kids. The slices were bigger now that Marília was dead.

The wake was in the living room where we slept, a white coffin, her little face, bruised up and purple, like a dead angel. The sight of her little socks, shoes, clothes, slowly realizing she would never wear them again. Never!

My mother is right, I should know more, but I can't remember. My sister Patricia may know more. She was supposed to watch Marília too.

[Suzana stands up to become Patricia]

Suzana and I were both supposed to watch Marília. But why should I care? Why should anyone care? Why are they feeling badly for my father? Why is my mother praising the stupid neighbor who dressed my brother in Marília's clothes? How dare she? My mother said it was Suzana's fault that Marília died, that if she had watched Marília, this would never have happened. I was horrified. Imagine having to handle this accusation … Suzana was only 13 when Marília died. Gosh, I admire, I respect my mother … But I avoid thinking that she might've known my father was molesting us and never did anything about it. [Pause]

People ask me, "How do you feel about it all?" I was 11 when she died. Marília's accident made me obsessively fearful about my own children; afraid when they crossed a street, when they played … petrified that some man might touch them or that they might perish under some stupid bus.

When my mother said that Suzana should be watching Marília; she was talking about me too, all of us … the only one she didn't blame was Millie. She's my mother's favorite. Millie is the eyewitness.

[Patricia sits and becomes Millie]

[*Millie is holding a Rosary*]

I was 7 years old. I was sitting next to my mother on the bus. After we got off, the bus threw Marília far onto the other side of the street. Had I crossed before the bus took off, my sister would be alive today. [*Pause*] When things began to settle, all I could think about was, what's next?

Lost in her grief; my mother refused to accept financial compensation from the company whose bus killed my sister. She said that receiving money for her daughter's death was unthinkable. I wish my mother had taken the money. Like many poor children, Marília died because a few cookies made a big difference.

Sometime after Marília died, Gladys, the sister between me and Marília, lost one of her eyes in an accident. Suzana got married and divorced after Rogério told her that her husband molested him for many years. That's when we sisters finally gathered the courage to talk about our father's secret. Rogério says that he spared Gladys because she had lost her eye. And here we are.

Yesterday, I came by my mother's place to see Rogério before he left for the airport. I missed him by a minute. He had gone to the store to buy candies, lots of candies to take home. I couldn't wait for him; I was late to church, but I left this Rosary for him, to keep him safe and happy going back home to New York.

[*Millie becomes R*]

Rosary

[R *picks up the rosary*]

The Rosary Millie gave me smells like roses; I loved it instantly! I said "good bye" to my mother ... I cried from the moment I left my mother's place until I arrived in Rio. Thank God Clara was there, waiting for me at the airport. She has been so comforting ... since college. Clara asked me how I felt after unburying my sister. Unburying Marília helped me understand my vulnerabilities as a child; the obsessive nature of my father's desires; my mother's and sisters' love for me ... my love of family. Clara hugged me ever so tightly: "My dear friend, inside your sister's grave you found the fabulous person you are today ... all the little girls whose hair you've cut, all the mothers and daughters you've counseled, the sister you have been to so many of us ... you are all of them!" Then my Clara left. The plane took off on time! I slept all night!

This morning, still on the plane, I woke up with light coming brightly through the window; my stomach was tight; my breath so shallow ... Gradually we approached the earth ... Images of Marília's remains taking over my mind, my thoughts, my senses ... I contemplated the mystery of Jesus' *Resurrection,* his welcoming my sister to life everlasting ... the Holy Spirit *Descending* upon Marília. My sister's *Ascension* to heaven ... [*Puts Rosary down*] I looked outside the window: the foamy ocean water coming to view. We landed on American soil, *my* home! Inside J. F. Kennedy Airport, I walked toward the American Citizen line, leaving behind young Brazilians whose lives are a mystery to me ... What type of visa do they have?

What jobs will they get? Are they going to stay and become ...
what? I felt the ribbon around my wrist ... so many wishes
fulfilled, so many to come ...

Marília's Lullaby

[Talks to "shrouded" Marília as she is gently placed in the
suitcase]

My Sweet Sister Marília

Where did you go?
Leaving me here,
So lonely a boy
Without you

I went to school
Learned about the earth
The turns it takes
There you disappeared

You left me here
Without direction
To join you; how?
Where are you?

Have you left?
I never let you
Held you closely
Made my chest cry

My most darling [Puts Marília in suitcase]
I'll forever miss you
But you stay no more
I'm letting you go

You deserve to rest
Sweet sister, Marília [Closes suitcase]
Go, go to heaven [Throws a kiss in the air meant to go to
M in heaven]
On earth no more

[Projection #32: Marília's photo]

[Projection #32 fades]

Black out!

PART TWO

Anti-Oppression and Healing in the Arts

1

Oppression and Prejudice Depicted in Biographical Drama and Performance

This chapter introduces evidence of how xenophobia, racism, homophobia, transphobia, and poverty can contribute to overall oppression and internalization of oppressive messages. Here, I use passages from *Marília* to demonstrate the usefulness of dramatic text and performance in shedding light on and promoting critical reflections on these issues.

Socioeconomic Issues and Prejudice as Tools of Oppression

There is inconsistency in the extant literature as to how prejudice, also referred to as "isms" here and elsewhere, is defined as forms or types of oppression (Arandjelović, 2023; Glick & Fiske, 1999; Jones et al., 2017), including many of those highlighted in my one-play, *Marília*, whose text appears in Part I of this book. The list of *isms* described in the extant literature is endless; however, those descriptions seem to have one thing in common—they underscore discriminatory practices meant to denigrate natural characteristics of the human body (e.g., skin color, aging skin) and/or criminalize people that ruling classes deem to be engaged in sins or unacceptable behaviors (e.g., gender phobia, sexual orientation), and/or blame vulnerable groups for their own vulnerabilities (e.g., poverty, houselessness). These vulnerabilities would not exist if not for the persistent oppression from the greedy ruling classes.

In *Marília*, I portray the sentiments and the realities that my family and I faced as we had to navigate dire poverty during the dictatorship in Brazil. In my storytelling narrative, I use dramatic language and props, a heuristic device to encompass some specific forms of prejudice (Speer, 2015)—they are xenophobia, racism, homophobia, and transphobia. I also show how such prejudices affected my life as I also faced poverty and classism. I wish to underscore that the experience of sexual molestation described in *Marília*, like other forms of abuse, is compounded by all manners of oppression and prejudice. Child sexual molestation, like myriad other inappropriate behaviors (e.g., rape, forced sex work) perpetrated by the oppressor, oftentimes family members, can have deleterious effects on physical health, mental health, and well-being. An individual's genetic constitution and its manifestations in human beings are not our choices. No one is born wanting to be hated, oppressed, or ostracized for being who they are.

In *Marília*, I emphasize the intersectional non-additive attributes (Dworkin, 2005) that affected my individual behaviors and social interactions. *Marília* was never meant to conjure up every possible form of oppression, but it was meant to explore specific forms of oppression and their internalization by the protagonist. Therefore, later in this chapter, I use examples and passages from *Marília* to demonstrate the effects of xenophobia, racism, homophobia, transphobia, poverty, and sexual molestation in my own life. But first is a summary of the literature showing the deleterious impact of these myriad *isms,* how we often internalize lies and misinformation about our own identities, and how people with intersecting attributes, such as myself, are more likely to be ignored and mistreated by structurally oppressive systems, like governments and their health programs.

Impacts of Oppression

The direct impact of oppression is difficult to measure, and this problem is compounded by the fact that myriad effects of oppression can also be associated with internalized oppression. Therefore, to understand oppression, it is also necessary to focus on its relationship to internalized oppression. For example, as human beings, we all should be paid fair wages. Some American citizens and the politicians that they support carry on rhetoric that citizens deserve better wages than immigrants for performing the same work because they are born in the United States. The practice of paying less for the same work is a form of oppression. An immigrant's belief and normalization of this rhetoric is the outcome of internalized oppression. There is a distinctly cognitive component to experiences of internalized oppression. For example, Pheterson (1986) notes that internalized oppression occurs when individuals within an oppressed group adopt and accept the prejudices and negative beliefs held about them by the dominant society. More recently, David et al. (2019) suggested that, for example, internalized racism is the act of turning the distress caused by societal oppression against oneself, one's family, and one's community.

Internalized oppression leads to experiences of power-lessness, isolation, self-doubt, self-invalidation, self-hatred, and fear (Padilla, 2001). For example, it manifests in how we assign importance to some beauty standards (e.g., blonde straight hair) and not others (Pinkney, 2014). The classic doll studies by Clark and Clark (1947, cited in David et al., 2019), one of the earliest studies of internalized racism, showed that one's internalization of inferiority starts at a very young age. As a result, oppressed people may develop a desire to distance themselves from their own racial or ethnic identity and adopt the behaviors or values of the oppressor, whose way of life is viewed as superior (Freire, 2000).

Internalized oppression also leads to experiences of alienation, both from oneself and from others. According to Pheterson (1986), internalized domination limits one's flourishing as it suppresses key elements of human relationships, such as empathy, trust, love, and openness. Here, oppression operates by promoting self-alienation and degradation of human development. Tappan (2006) suggests that internalized oppression ought not to be understood from a simplistic psychological perspective but as a sociocultural phenomenon. Akin to Freire, Tappan theorizes that both internalized domination (i.e., superiority) and internalized oppression (i.e., inferiority) are experienced as alienation because both require the denial of reality, and such alienation limits the emotional spectrum and flourishing of both dominator and dominated.

The impact of myriad tools of oppression targeting already marginalized groups of people is well documented in the literature. For example, people who report experiences of racism also report increased levels of stress. Racism-related stress arises from exposure to everyday microaggressions, contextual stress (e.g., joblessness), and intergenerational transmission of discrimination. Racism-related stress is associated with various health outcomes, including maladaptive coping mechanisms such as excessive cigarette smoking, hypertension, and cardiovascular reactivity, and it hampers one's ability and inclination to trust, form close relationships, and engage in social groups (Brondolo et al., 2012; Harrell, 2000). Another example is internalized transphobia, which is associated with reduced life satisfaction (Cronon et al., 2019), self-esteem (Austin & Goodman, 2017), and high levels of depression, anxiety, and somatization (Bockting et al., 2020). These may heighten other negative outcomes, from difficulty in finding employment to suicidal ideation (Mizock & Mueser, 2014).

It is crucial to shed light on *internalized dominance*, a belief system that fosters privilege for those already in power on marginalized (Hitchcock, 2002; Tappan, 2006). For example, Hitchcock (2002) argues that white people's relationship with people of color is often defined by white people's purported fear of people of color, along with experiences of superiority (Tappan, 2006; Tochluk, 2013; Wake, 2022). Another example, within a heterosexist society, it has been posited that heterosexual people are largely unaware of their social and economic privileges compared to people under the LGBTQIA+ umbrella (DiAngelo, 1997). Nonetheless, homophobia, often flaunted by heterosexual people, has been shown to be linked to higher HIV infection rates, depression, substance misuse, and domestic violence (Frye et al., 2019; Jeffries et al., 2013), and hate crimes against LGBTQAI+ people (Federal Bureau of Investigation [FBI], 2019).

Oppression in *Marília*

In writing and performing *Marília*, I learned how key pieces of my identity came together to create a self that is full of conflicts and contradictions. I came to see that, even though I had learned a lot about the structural issues created to hamper my development into a full human being during my formative years, I had also internalized lies perpetuated by oppressive ruling classes that influenced negatively my early years in Brazil and also in the United States as an adult. Below, I define key forms of prejudice and oppression that I have expressed in *Marília* in a manner that was made possible by my understanding and action against internalized oppression. Here I use text, photography, and sculptures to underscore how different art forms can be used for similar purpose. The art seen here was created for the the *Realm of Dead*, and adaptation of *Marília* (Pinto, 2022c).

Xenophobia, Racism, and Colorism

Xenophobia has been defined as a form of discrimination against people from countries other than the one where they were born (Sundstrom & Kim, 2014). Xenophobia is often expressed alongside racism, which has been defined as a system of advantage bestowed on people with lighter skin colors, plus prejudiced attitudes and discrimination against people with darker skin tones (Rothenberg, 2004). Colorism is a form of racism that can occur within the same racial/ethnic group, a social phenomenon highly prevalent in Brazil (Devulsky, 2021), where I was born and grew up. Colorism can be experienced even within groups of immigrants from the same country of origin.

In *Marília*, I demonstrate how I came to understand the difficulties I, and scores of immigrants from the Global South, face upon arrival in the United States and for the duration of our lives as immigrants. Oppressive classes use legal and social obstacles hampering immigrants' flourishing to ostracize and even demonize immigrants of color. The following passage from *Marília* illustrates how I used the conflict to situate the immigrant in this context.

> PROTAGONIST: "Immigrants from poor countries come here under difficult conditions: terrible debts; some swim across dangerous waters, and others may die of heatstroke or suffocation in shipping containers. After all that, we'll happily do any job we can get, no matter where we come from."

Furthermore, the following text and its accompanying picture, projected on a screen during the performance, show how, by using drama and humor, a performer can shine light on myriad prejudices and show how internalized oppression can be extricated.

PROTAGONIST: "After my initial job adventures, I looked for work at the *Daily News*. I found an ad that said: *"Looking for easy going hairdresser, comfortable cutting hair of both men and women"* ... *"Hairdresser should have a cosmetology license and be fluent in English."* After only five months in New York, this, I definitely could not manage! But I called the place anyway and made an appointment for an interview. This was a "Marília" moment when she enables me to do things I could never do on my own. I was nervous; my English was good enough to survive but not to understand details and clients' preferences about their hair ... In my interview, I was polite and answered truthfully each question ... but I did not disclose that my visa to stay in the United States was about to expire. When I went for my job interview, I was about to become an 'illegal alien' ... a threat to the United States of America! I was fearful that I could be deported." [*Projection of the protagonist's passport picture altered to evoke an extraterrestrial being, not human*]

The internalization of oppression like xenophobia and one's identity as an immigrant often disrupts the immigrant ability to adapt and thrive in the country to which we migrate. Intrapersonal and interpersonal conflicts can cause people within a marginalized group to think poorly of themselves and the people within their communities. We begin to act on the negative perceptions that society has of us (Padilla, 2001). Internalized oppression, as a result of one's status as an immigrant, dovetails with internalized racism/colorism expressed by the pursuit of whiteness by changing one's physical appearance (e.g., blonde hair, skin-lightening products) and by internalizing mainstream ideals and goals. For example, Brazilians and other immigrants alike often avoid using their native idioms in professional settings for fear of punishment, ridicule (e.g., accents), and out of shame.

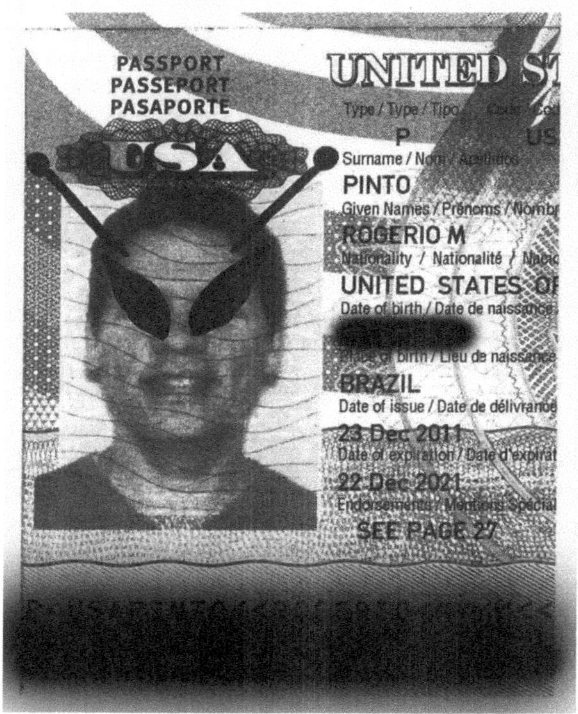

FIGURE 1.1 *Alien*
Artwork by Rogério M. Pinto depicts a mundane form of identification, the American passport, doctored to suggest that it belongs to an extraterrestrial being.

Internalized xenophobia and racism are often compounded by undocumented immigration status. This may result in feelings of inferiority because immigrants often pursue unreachable standards of beauty, language, and cultural norms that undermine their own (David et al., 2019). As they are ostracized, immigrants facing xenophobia and racism may come to see the oppressor as superior and tragically begin to see themselves as less than human (Chavis & Johnson, 2023). The above passage from *Marília* illustrates how drama and performance can be used to demonstrate how the feelings and beliefs coming from internalized oppression can be overcome. It thus succeeds in fulfilling a key goal of personal narrative that supports self-determination and liberatory action as the protagonist reveals sociopolitical and economic sources of oppression, a key strategy both Freire and Boal used in their teachings.

Homophobia and Transphobia

The term "homophobia" has been used in academia and in social circles alike to describe and sometimes explain different types of discrimination (e.g., within families, job-related) against people whose identities fall under the LGBTQIA+ umbrella (Herek, 2004). Internalized homophobia leads to mental health issues, physical health disparities, and difficulties with romantic relationships (David, 2013). Myriad cognitive effects may come from being around and/or targeted by homophobic individuals, from feeling doomed, wrong, sinful, and/or a "bad" person whose romantic relationships are not as good or stable as heterosexual ones. This may prevent people under the LGBTQIA+ umbrella from developing intimate relationships with partners.

In *Marília,* I share with my audiences my experiences of homophobia toward me, starting with my mother when I was a child and how that type of experience persisted in my life as I grew up and began to interface with various sectors of society. I also depict how, at some points in my development, I internalized homophobic messages, as follows.

PROTAGONIST: "I remember my mother asking the
doctor, "Why is my son so much like his sister, why all
his friends are girls, why is he feisty and yet so sensitive,
is he normal, my son?" [*Projection of the protagonist*

FIGURE 1.2 *Drag*
Photo by Eva Muller depicting the protagonist in drag. The details of the costume include shells and feathers evoking Brazilian carnaval themes and natural beauty.

in a carnaval costume à la drag queen to add a moment of relaxed fun used to underscore the seriousness of the text that followed]

PROTAGONIST CONTINUES: "My mother's preoccupations haunted me all my life and made me fearful about my future ... In college, I was under the impression that I could never be a successful biologist because I wasn't "manly" enough ... when I was in college, there was no LGBT liberation yet. No transgender liberation in sight! Being feminine and having a boy's body, I feared I'd be beat up and killed by bigots and the military police. There were voices from my childhood echoing inside my head over and over and over ... *Bichinha*! *Mulherzinha*! *Veado*! Sissy! Little girl! Faggot! These voices were meant to drown me."

As indicated at the end of this passage, I also share with my audiences how, at present, I have a better understanding of how I internalized those negative messages. The phrase "These voices were meant to drown me" demonstrates a different level of awareness about the world about me, what Freire called critical consciousness. In the play, I hoped that this entire sequence might serve as inspiration for critical dialogues audience members might have about their own trajectory navigating moments of homophobia, internalization of hateful messages, and coming to some understanding that they are human beings and thus deserving of flourishing regardless of their sexual orientations. I also hope that heterosexual individuals in the audience might imagine what it means to be gay in a society that is homophobic, and think about their own (or lack of) empathy toward people under the LGBTQIA+ umbrella.

In a paper that I wrote with colleagues in 2024, based on the extant literature, I contended that homophobia is a threat to individual and public health as it predicts violent, often fatal behaviors toward gay men, transgender women, nonbinary individuals, and others under the LGBTQIA+ umbrella. We showed that by following Freire's blueprint for critical dialogues, we used illustrations to evoke conversations around heteronormativity, homosexuality, and gender roles among heterosexual men. We showed that during critical dialogues, the men developed critical reflections around their homophobic attitudes and behaviors (Pinto et al., 2024). I bring up this study in this context because it provides evidence that heterosexual men, the group most likely to perpetrate violent homophobic acts, can improve tolerance and empathy toward LGBTQIA+ by having critical dialogues about deep-seated attitudes about the superiority of heterosexuality and masculinity. Likewise, I used drama and performance around the text above to achieve similar results.

The term "transphobia" is often used to refer to discrimination against people who identify as transgender, gender nonconforming, and/or nonbinary. It has been defined in strong language as "disgust toward individuals not conforming to society's gender expectations." Similarly to homophobia, such "disgust" is often expressed through harassment, violence, and discrimination (Bandini & Maggi, 2014).

Because people are assigned a sex at birth, when that sex does not match the self-perceived gender identity of the person to whom it has been assigned, this situation can become a source of dread, anxiety, and a sense of loneliness for many trans/nonbinary-identified people (Austin, 2016; Markman, 2011). Gender identity fluidly develops over time, and people have cognitive capacities to fully understand how to achieve the body transformations they need to match their emotional and developmental expectations (Pinto et al., 2008). The notion that sex and/or gender can be assigned at birth, a blatant form of oppression, comes from the pervasive cultural understanding of sex and gender as identities that exist only in a binary state, thus making it harder for people who do not identify with one or the other category (male or female) to achieve full status as a human being (Markman, 2011). The binary categorization of gender is a tool of oppression by which transphobia is maintained and justified, while it also privileges heterosexuality by maintaining a heteronormative society that vilifies all other gender identities and sexual orientations outside of the "normal" binary range.

In *Marília,* I introduce the type of violence to which people under the LGBTQIA+ umbrella are exposed in day-to-day life. The passage below, though not directly related to the oppression of a transgender identity, shows how drama can be used to build momentum by introducing a happy realization that is then frustrated by a conflict. Practitioners of the theater of the oppressed often use this technique. Here, I use it in connection with the text below, where I expose my mother's assumptions about a binary world where there are only two genders. The passage echoes the text above about the internalized hateful voices I still hear as an adult.

> PROTAGONIST: "My next job was in construction; imagine that! Surprisingly, I did well putting up drywall, painting … you know, butch stuff. But it didn't last long … one of the guys on that site attacked me. I was having lunch. He appeared out of nowhere. Like the bullies from my childhood, he called me names and then spread a patching compound all over my face. I couldn't see a thing! The construction workers on the site helped me get out and wash my face, but I never went back there. I was scared!"

This scene depicts what the protagonist experienced as an adult, and here, I show a level of awareness that it is not available to a child for developmental reasons. The text depicted below illustrates how my mother's messages about binary gender identity come to an unfortunate episode of transphobia that non-binary people face in their day-to-day lives. Here, I also expose the racist messages that I had received about having curly hair. Oppressive messages are not only about one thing or another; they are often layered with nuances of myriad *isms* like classism, racism, and sexism.

> PROTAGONIST: " … when my sister Gladys was getting married … I let my hair grow a bit longer so that I could get a new style for the wedding. Oh God! My long hair looked beautiful! As the hairdresser blew my hair with the big round brush, a miracle was taking place before my very eyes. My hair was straight! … Growing up, I had learned that straight hair was good and curly hair was bad. You had either good or bad hair, and mine was bad! I felt that my *straight*

hair could save my life! I couldn't wait to show my mother … when she saw 'the hair that could save my life,' … she was furious, '*Ficou parecendo uma puta*!' My new hair made me look like a whore, she said! Some part of me enjoyed what she said … she imagined me as a woman! … that day, I was afraid of her. She called *me* a whore! I ended up getting a haircut I knew would appease my mother … However, a few days later, I told her, '*Nunca mais a senhora ou qualquer pessoa vai decidir qualquer coisa a respeito do my cabelo, meu gênero or como eu deva viver a minha vida*!' Never again will you or anyone else decide anything about my looks, my gender, or how I should live my life!"

In this scene, I show how the protagonist can expose different forms of oppression (i.e., transphobia and racism), question one's sense of doubt from internalized oppression (i.e., getting a haircut), and then come through the scene with some awareness that helps the protagonist act against that oppression (i.e., refusal to let anyone decide what is best for the protagonist). From this type of drama, one can explore how internalized transphobia may be the result of cognitive beliefs about not being enough of a "man" or a "woman" (Bockting et al., 2020; Scandurra et al., 2018). Questioning one's own sense of self instead of society's cruel oppression is a common cognitive distortion that reflects the internalization of stigma toward transgender people (Rood et al., 2017). Children need to believe what their caretakers will keep them safe and cared for. During childhood, most oppressive messages take hold in our consciousness, a time in which we cannot discern right from wrong, true from false, or the in-between permutations of morally charged dichotomies. Though we may internalize oppression at any moment of our lives, I believe that in childhood, we are most vulnerable to lies and misinformation, and the more lies and misinformation we hear as children, the more prone we will be to believe in those lies and glorify misinformation as adults.

Poverty

Poverty has been defined as a lack of access to economic capital (Wagle, 2002). It affects people's decision-making processes because people living in poverty face numerous obstacles that hamper their abilities to flourish, such as insecure and unsafe housing, houselessness, and hunger. These experiences have been linked to difficulty learning new skills and succeeding at developmental tasks (Sheehy-Skeffington & Rea, 2017). People living in poverty are also less likely to perceive that their actions will affect how their lives will turn out. People living in poverty endorse experiences of social exclusion due to stereotypes and stigmas related to being poor (Sheehy-Skeffington & Rea, 2017). Poverty adversely affects well-being as it causes stress and negative emotional states, such as depression, which hampers a person's ability to escape poverty (Haushofer & Fehr, 2014). These factors may create a feedback loop that perpetuates experiences of poverty.

In *Marília*, I introduce the complications of having minimal living space for a family of ten and how the closeness may provide opportunities for sexual abuse, discussed below.

PROTAGONIST: "I came from a housing project in Belo Horizonte. There, we played barefoot on the dirt, grass, and unpaved streets. A long avenue connected the nine buildings to the center of the city … We lived on the first floor of building number Four. Marília's accident took place at the bus stop in front of that building. From the building's open courtyard, we could see inside each apartment. We knew one another's intimate business. The police often raided the buildings without any apparent reason. Growing up under the dictatorship, lack of privacy was commonplace. Ten of us lived in a tiny two-bedroom apartment: me, my mother and father, my brothers and sisters, and the little pet rabbit. I slept in the same bed with my two younger sisters, Gladys and Millie." [*Projection of Housing Project*]

FIGURE 1.3 *Housing Project*
Photo by Rogério M. Pinto depicting housing project where the protagonist grew up in the 1960s and 1970s.

PROTAGONIST: "I feel so heavy … heavy and old … old and fat! Do I look fat? Growing up, I was so skinny, a scrawny kid! There was never enough food. My mother and siblings worked hard all day to feed all of us … Alone all day, I would open the refrigerator hoping to find food I knew wasn't there, adjusting to the fact that the refrigerator was empty, the house was empty. I would close the refrigerator and feel utterly disappointed even though I already knew there was nothing there. I always hoped I'd find candies … lots of candies! [*Projection of bunches of candies to evoke the eish to have them in one's life*]

Poverty is much more than lacking the "things" we need to flourish or wish to have to feel secure in our existence as humans. Poverty is a widespread global experience fraught with complex socioeconomic experiences that the ruling classes and governments try very hard to hide. Nobody wants to be poor and go without the basic necessities of life. In *Marília*, I use my sister's death, a tragic event in a poor family's life, to explore issues of safety, hunger, and house insecurity, but also to examine the meaning of hope and joy in the mind of a child as the protagonist finishes a monologue about being hungry hoping to find candy in an otherwise empty refrigerator.

Here, I use Freire's reflections on what it means to be poor and oppressed and Boal's application of hope and frustration to challenge the audience to become more aware of socioeconomic conditions that influence how we live and how we feel.

Sexual Molestation

I have added the subject matter of sexual molestation here because it is a form of oppression at the interpersonal level. It is also important to understand sexual molestation in Marília

FIGURE 1.4 *Candies*
Rogerio M. Pinto's artwork. Two stacked suitcases, filled with candies and cookies, celebrate his journey from Brazil to the United States, from hunger to sustenance. (Photo by Emerson Granillo)

within the sociopolitical and economic context highlighted above. I am using the term "sexual molestation" here to refer to non-consensual intimate emotional and/or sexual relations between family members. As portrayed in *Marília*, survivors of sexual molestation often report feeling shame and self-blame for abusive behaviors toward them, many of which may have occurred at a moment in their lives when they did not have the necessary developmental capacity even to understand what was happening to them. Oftentimes, survivors of sexual molestation cognitively internalize these experiences by blaming themselves instead of the perpetrator, by trying to shift the responsibility from the perpetrator's actions to themselves, by denying that the abusive contact even occurred, and by doubting the credibility of their memories (Shaked et al., 2021). In *Marília*, the impact of sexual molestation comes with self-doubt, gender confusion, and even love for the perpetrator, as follows.

> PROTAGANIST: "As a child, I thought what made a girl a girl was having a pussy. All my sisters had vaginas. If I had one, I'd be just like Marília, right? A Marília who never died. In my mind, everyone thought I might be a girl. I knew I was a girl, even though I didn't have a pussy. I began to wonder if my father also knew I was a girl … the way he looked at me … showed special interest in me … I was confused … you see, my father touched me intimately. His touch was firm and manly; he was a man. Therefore, I must be a "girl." Perhaps Marília? My father was so sad after she died … Maybe if I was Marília, could I make him happy again!?" [*Projection of a truck wrapped in chains securing the secrecy of incest*]

Though socially fraught with stigma and secrecy, sexual molestation is not in and of itself a form of *ism*, probably because it is only visible once it is revealed. People have asked me why I decided to reveal it in such a public way. I felt that I

FIGURE 1.5 *Father*
Rogerio M. Pinto's artwork. A black trunk standing on four legs wrapped in chains with the word "Pai" ("father") on it. A red bottom atop invites the viewer to click the button and shed light on the scene sexual molestation portrayed inside. (Photo by Emerson Granillo)

did not have a voice as a child. When I did, as an adult, I felt I needed to share the experiences hidden within my family. To my surprise, so many people have approached me to share their own experiences and to tell me how their interactions with *Marília* helped them reconfigure their thoughts and feelings around sexual molestation and trauma that comes with molestation. *Marília* evoked critical dialogues about the origin of sexual molestation and about the social implications of it. To my knowledge, neither Freire nor Boal specifically focused on sexual molestation in their writings. Nonetheless, it is only natural that this subject matter flowed from the myriad forms of oppression explored in *Marília*—one form of oppression begets other forms of oppression and, thus, more violence.

Grief and Loss

I am also adding here the subject matter of grief and loss related to death because this complex combination of social and personal experiences expresses itself differently under oppressive sociopolitical and economic conditions. *Marília* communicates with nineteenth-century Brazilian Romanticists (e.g., essayist Euclides da Cunha—1866–1909) who dwelt on morbidity and death, but who also introduced the notion of determinism in prose and poetry, evident in the struggles of my family around Marília's death. In *Marília*, audience members are encouraged to join the protagonist to converse with the spirit of his dead sister. A call to spirits for help is a common practice in Brazilian drama and performance, one that is influenced by Spiritism, a popular philosophy/religion founded by Allan Kardec (1804–69). According to this doctrine, humans have immortal spirits temporarily inhabiting the physical body—spirits may come back after death to dwell in the world of the living (Kardec, 1987).

How people respond to the death of a child when the entire family is living in poverty is very different compared to a family that has the resources for the "usual" and expected rituals around death, such as funeral and burial arrangements, all of which are very costly under the best circumstances. For example, when Marília, one of eight children, died when she was not even three years old, my family did not have a cemetery plot nor the money to buy one. Marília's funeral wake took place in the living room of the small apartment where we lived. The amount of grief and emotional pain experienced by all of us is partly expressed by the following lines from *Marília*.

PROTAGONIST: "Lost in her grief; my mother refused to accept financial compensation from the company whose bus killed my sister. She said that receiving money for her daughter's death was unthinkable. I wish my mother had taken the money. Like many poor children, Marília died because a few cookies made a big difference."

The loss of a child by death forces the entire family to adapt and cope with loss and grief. The literature suggests that the death of a sibling intensifies the psychological vulnerability of the entire family. Communication patterns, such as the one expressed above, influences how family members can survive the death of a child. My last line in the excerpt above also shows my resentment, one that I know I share with my siblings. How I use drama here, and elsewhere in my play, reflects Self-Presentation Theory (Goffman, 1959) in that I use text and performance to express issues concerning loss and grief alongside myriad sociopolitical and economic issues to audiences whose life experiences might have been very different from my own. As in the *Theatre of the Oppressed*, the performative drama in *Marília* included ingratiation, exemplification, and often a form of supplication (Jones & Pitman, 1982) for help aimed to bringing out conflict—my audience cannot save Marília or my family.

2

Arts-Based Methods for Critical Dialogues and Liberation

This chapter introduces how Freire's and Boal's theories and corresponding anti-oppression methods are interconnected and how we can use them to promote liberation through drama and performance regardless of what the sociopolitical and economic environment might be at any given time.

Critical consciousness is the globally known centerpiece of Freire's work, which has been widely used as the foundation for advancing social justice efforts and liberation. Freire believed that by engaging people in what he called community circles, those involved would reflect on the socioeconomic and political conditions around them and become inspired to act against oppression. This process presupposes that humans have intellectual and emotional capacities to observe, describe, reflect on, and comprehend the socioeconomic and political environment around them. It also presupposes that individuals can take both personal and collective action against myriad forms of oppression and prejudice (Freire, 2000; Watts, Diemer, & Voight, 2011), including those discussed in Chapter 1 and which I highlighted in connection to my play *Marília*.

Similarly to Freire, since the 1970s, other educators and researchers have relied on and studied the impact of art forms as aids to help marginalized and minoritized people engage in "critical dialogues." These critical dialogues are often guided by a set of "critical questions" that facilitate the "critical reflection" process, which can help critical dialogue participants improve their understanding of oppressive forces. The goal of critical dialogues is to enhance participation in civic and political "critical action."

Critical Dialogues: A critical dialogue, or a community circle, is a strategy that can be aided by questions that evoke analyses and reflections among participants in the conversation. The conversation is often about the socioeconomic and political conditions under which marginalized people live. Critical dialogues are often sparked using art forms such as images and illustrations aimed to tap people's innate curiosity ("curious disposition") to evaluate the roots and effects of privilege and oppression (Freire, 2000; Lewis, 2012). The goal of a critical dialogue is to help people engage in the process of critical reflection and critical action, the combination of which facilitates the development of critical consciousness.

Critical consciousness has been described by Freire and others as a process and not an outcome. The way we develop critical consciousness is not the same for everyone. It is influenced by a person's life experiences and inclination to act against oppression (Freire, 2000; Jemal & Bussey, 2018; Lewis, 2012). People may experience critical consciousness differently at various points in their lives, and they may temporarily or permanently lose hold of it. The extant literature shows that critical reflection and critical action are not necessarily empirically linked (Frye et al., 2019; Shin et al., 2018). In other words, a person can engage in critical dialogues and reflection, but they do not always participate immediately in civic or political action after critical dialogue and reflection. However, engagement in various types of critical dialogues at different moments in a person's life may, over time, encourage action which is the process for the development of critical consciousness.

I made several of these points in an article published with colleagues aimed at demonstrating how, by using iconic illustrations in critical dialogues, we were able to help heterosexual men reflect on and improve their attitudes around homophobia and sexism (Pinto et al., 2024a). Being cross-sectional, the study in question was not meant to show actions that might have been taken after reflection; however, during critical dialogues, participants showed interest and willingness to help combat homophobia and sexism. Interest and willingness to act are precursors of "critical action." To see the image that we used to facilitate critical dialogues and understand the process the men went through, please see Pinto et al. (2024a).

Arts in Education and the Public Sphere

Freire used different forms of artistic expression, including pictographs, tiles, and sculptures representing day-to-day living under oppressive circumstances during what came to be called community circles or critical dialogues. Freire and others documented how art forms used to spark critical dialogues helped participants show personal vulnerability and empathy toward themselves and others. Building on Freire's work, Boal (2006), the pioneer of the *Theatre of the Oppressed*, contended that visual (e.g., theatrical properties) and theatrical methods could spark conversations with the potential to help marginalized people imagine/conceive a world that could be free of oppression. Since Freire developed the concept of critical consciousness, for the past fifty years, educators and researchers have used a variety of art forms to spark critical dialogues—for example, rap music and videos, photography, storytelling, and illustrations (Carlson, Engebretson, & Chamberlain, 2006; Fiddian-Green et al., 2019; Pinto et al., 2024a; Watts & Abdul-Adil, 1998; Watts et al., 2002).

Since its initial development by Freire in the 1970s, the concept of critical consciousness remains a relevant topic of research and practice across various disciplines, including childhood development (Heberle, Rapa, & Farago, 2020), social justice (Kumagai & Lypson, 2009), and education (Cervantes-Soon et al., 2017). Teachers and social justice practitioners across the globe have used didactic and dramatic techniques that evolved over time, but which were founded in the *Pedagogy of the Oppressed* and *Theatre of the Oppressed*. Programs to help marginalized and minoritized people develop critical consciousness abound. A burgeoning literature shows that critical consciousness can be integrated into different subject matters, such as mathematics (Stephan et al., 2021), biology (Bernal-Munera, 2023), social work (Barak, 2016), and art education (Mernick, 2021). For the purpose of this book and this chapter, I will help us to focus on the role that the concepts at hand—i.e., critical dialogue, reflection, action, and consciousness—play in art education and public art. The main reason for this focus is that a rich literature exists on these topics, which directly relate to my expertise in social work research, education and practice, and art-making for public consumption.

As a professor of social work and a practicing artist, I have created most of my artworks, research, and teaching to help me achieve the goal of assisting people to engage in critical dialogues and reflection, the precursors of critical consciousness. My work involves creating or identifying artworks with the potential to spark dialogues that can lead to reflection and action toward liberation and the advancement of diversity, equity, and inclusion (DEI). For example, to explore how artistic and social science research can be integrated and how different art forms can together spark critical dialogues, I created and performed *Realm of the Dead*: A multimedia art

FIGURE 2.1 Realm of the Dead: *A multimedia art installation Photo by Marc Arthur depicting the aerial view of the Realm of the Dead installation at the University of Michigan School of Social Work. The sculptures represent the graves of the children's section of a public cemetery. Note: This photo also appears in Pinto, R. M. (2022c). Realm of the Dead: A Mixed-Media Installation Performance. Ground Works. https://groundworks. io/journal.* © 2022 by Rogério Meireles Pinto is licensed under *CC-BY-NC-ND 4.0. https://doi.org/10.48807/2022.0.0105*

installation, the results of which I published after I had given several performances (Pinto, 2022c).

Realm of the Dead was based on an adaptation of *Marília*. In *Realm of the Dead,* the protagonist delivers a sixty-minute monologue on a forty-foot-square white floor representing the cemetery where Marília was buried. The installation included thirty-five assemblage sculptures built in and around vintage suitcases and trunks of all sizes (see Figure 2.1 above). As an installation performance open to the public and free of charge, at the imagined cemetery depicted in the *Realm of the Dead,* graves stood six feet apart to adhere to the original COVID-19 prevention guidelines still in place in 2021. A maximum of three to four audience participants stood at each grave or "stations," which evoked the *Via Dolorosa,* the symbolic path of Jesus's crucifixion.

Realm of the Dead audience participants moved from station to station as one would in a spiritual pilgrimage. An altar bell used during the blessing of the host during the mass in Catholic churches signaled audience participants to advance to the next station at the end of each monologue. Many monologues underscored the collusion between the Catholic Church and the Brazilian State that was in power during the Brazilian dictatorship. *Realm of the Dead* audience members indicated a growth in their knowledge and awareness around the key prejudices and issues dramatized in the show, including xenophobia, homophobia and transphobia, poverty, and sexual trauma. In the words of an audience member, "Moving around the room, kneeling, moving closer, crouching, peering through holes, examining things closely was impactful."

Cultural Critical Consciousness

Most of what we know about the nature of critical consciousness comes from the extant literature that investigates the role of the arts in the education of young people. From the art teacher's perspective, the balance between visual representations and students' lived experiences is crucial to evoking critical dialogues.

> **Cultural Critical Consciousness.** The literature of the past two decades has tried to reinvent critical consciousness by developing the concept of "cultural critical consciousness," which means the ability to analyze artistic elements from the unique perspective of one's culture (Gay & Kirkland, 2003). Such analysis has been suggested to help people develop what has been referred to as cultural identities.

The origin of cultural critical consciousness, a contemporary understanding of Freire's critical consciousness, appears to have started by art teachers who believed that critical dialogues could be helpful in unearthing the value orientations of both teachers and students. This process can help students learn different subjects while understanding their positionalities in the world ("culture"), such as where they live, where they go to school, and where they interact with their communities and families. Gay and Kirkland (2003) argue that a major component of preparing educators to teach should be personal and professional critical consciousness about racial, cultural, and ethnic diversity—these are issues that I explored in both *Marília* and in its adaption, *Realm of the Dead*, above.

Critical dialogues, those that focus on self-examination and understanding of personal and cultural values, call for diverse social identities—e.g., racial/ethnic, gender, social class—among critical dialogue participants. This is true both in the classroom and in the broader community. These critical dialogues need to be guided by experienced facilitators trained in methods that can facilitate authentic language, life-based examples, and discussion concerning factual sociopolitical and economic circumstances (Pinto et al., 2024b). Beyond the classroom setting, where art has been used as a springboard for critical dialogues, these have been referred to as a form of critical public pedagogy (Zorrilla & Tisdell, 2016). For this type of critical dialogue, public art has often been used to encourage critical reflection and direct civic and political action (Ozga, 2016). In these instances, participants in critical dialogues in public settings are invited to question who they are in the present, then to ask themselves what they represent in different historic contexts and vis-à-vis their current socioeconomic and political environment. This type of critical dialogue, cultivating reflection and action, is more likely to generate critical consciousness among participants.

The setting of critical dialogues among young people is often framed by the art teacher. Expectedly, the extant literature illustrates how the development of critical consciousness can be embedded into the work of any teacher, including those teaching adult learners, regardless of the subject matter being taught. For example, authors of a study set in Zimbabwe discuss how the development of critical consciousness within art teacher education programs could be useful in addressing the intersection of gender, art, and education (Dziwa, Postma, & Combrink, 2022). The programs under analysis aimed to help students develop critical consciousness around complex issues concerning gender beliefs and attitudes. The authors found that all female participants demonstrated a heightened understanding of oppressive gender inequality and imbalance.

As key elements in their students' potential to develop critical consciousness, Dziwa et al. (2022) cited the facilitators of critical dialogues' abilities to reflect on their own values and to empower their students. Much research is still needed to generate empirical evidence on the myriad ways that the critical dialogue facilitator can influence consciousness, the result of reflection and action. A few considerations around this area of research can be found in Pinto et al. (2024a)—for example, the facilitator's capacity to follow a predetermined critical dialogue protocol and the need for training facilitators to help essential participants of dialogue not to offend each other with prejudicial statements concerning myriad marginalized social identities of critical dialogue participants.

For another example, concerning adults' capacity to develop critical consciousness around issues related to gender and sexual orientation oppressions, see Pinto et al. (2024a). Using empirical data, here, the authors demonstrate how the process of critical reflection took place among eleven critical dialogues among men with histories of incarceration and substance use. The authors relied on an illustration that depicted day-to-day scenes concerning the lives of LGBTQIA2+ people to engage men with intersecting minoritized identities in critical dialogues. Facilitators helped the men confront prejudices and biased attitudes toward people whose identities differed from their own. The authors identified distinct stages of critical dialogues, discussions threads—*Descriptions*, *Explanations*, *Interpretations*, and *Implications*—that arose from the illustration they used. The authors showed how, by going through these discussion threads, participants developed states of heightened awareness of the oppressive nature of homophobia and sexism. This is the first empirical work showing critical dialogue discussion threads and the process of critical reflection around homophobia and sexism. This model can now be used to engage people of different social identities to try this type of exercise.

Public Art, Critical Dialogues, and Social Consciousness

As the *Realm of the Dead* suggests, the classroom is not the exclusive setting for critical dialogue. It is recommended that public art forms used to facilitate critical dialogues, be it temporary or permanent, be environment-specific. To evoke civic and/or political engagement, the art form (e.g., sculpture, mural, photographs) ought to convey a local sensibility. Local, permanent, or temporary public art often provides an opportunity for viewers and listeners (e.g., spontaneous music and theater) to enjoy the experience while confronting past and contemporary histories, local politics, and socioeconomic issues that may have and still may be influencing their lives and the lives of family and friends. Based on his teachings around *Theatre of the Oppressed* methods, Boal suggested that, in order to help audiences engage in critical dialogue and reflection, theater "spectators" need to be invited to become active participants in the aesthetics and outcomes of theater-making. This premise holds true in relationship to all art forms in that people who are engaged with any art form may discuss their feelings and observations with other viewers and listeners, take these discussions to their families and friends, and then further develop critical reflection and behaviors toward critical consciousness. The techniques used to help audiences engage with different art forms may vary, of course, but the call for audience interaction and dialogues remains our best strategy toward liberation.

> **Social Consciousness.** The literature suggests that exploration of the arts has been shown to improve people's critical thinking skills outside the formal classroom setting. Furthermore, public art in Europe, the Americas, Asia, and others has been shown to generate opportunities for informal dialogue, alternative forms of inquiry and improved social consciousness—collective consciousness that we share as members of society and of our communities. Social consciousness stems from shared social identities which foster empathy toward one another.

For example, Ozga (2016) used case studies of site-specific artworks to study photograph installations and their potential to foster critical reflection and what I referred to as "social consciousness" above (Pavlidis, 2015). Ozga examines myriad art forms, murals, montages, backlit displays, and object integration, and then suggests that perhaps the combination of myriad art forms (like the *Realm of the Dead*) and not one art form or another is what invites interaction and critical dialogue. Public art also creates possibilities for those experiencing it to question how the art to which one is being exposed was made and the history behind art-making. In a book entitled *Street Art and Democracy in Latin America*, Dabène (2020) explores the contributions of street art toward democracy in Bogota (Colombia), São Paulo (Brazil), Valparaiso (Chile), Oaxaca (Mexico), and Havana (Cuba). Dabène explains that when artists feel empowered to take over certain public spaces, they use those spaces to create art that depicts rage and messages concerning the negative effects of prejudices, social ills, and political repression.

Artists involved in creating public works of art successfully raise public awareness, nurture public debates, and hold politicians and policymakers accountable. Dabène, for example, provides an innovative analysis of how artists, supported by people who experience local public art, can gather support for civic and political action when public spaces containing art are confronted by oppressors who wish to repress and/ or eliminate public art. By engaging in democratic dialogues, artists and local authorities can engage in actions inspired by what has been called "street-level democracy," a form of governance that, in this case, arises directly from the influences of public art.

Developmental Considerations

The examples above, and how art can be experienced by people in general, are not age specific as they speak to art that can be seen, heard, felt, and experienced by anyone who happens to be around it. However, I wish to point out that people in different developmental stages have different capacities to understand art and thus engage in the process of critical consciousness. Nonetheless, any human being can experience art in their homes, the street, the classroom, or the library. Despite their ages or where they experience art, anyone can engage, to different degrees, in some form of dialogue to explore socioeconomic, cultural, or economic issues that may or may not influence their critical consciousness (reflection and action). Arts in education or the public arena can help those experiencing it to challenge power relations, confront and change one's own assumptions about themselves, their peers, and society. Being that critical dialogues depend on speaking and listening, other forms of communication may be needed to influence the development of consciousness. Though research is still lacking in this area, the extant literature, particularly in the areas of drama and performance, has suggested different spaces and forms of communication that may help to galvanize dialogue and consciousness. Therefore, below, I introduce the background of the *Theater of the Oppressed* and its capacity to help with critical dialogue, reflection, action, and consciousness.

Theatre of the Oppressed and Other Current Approaches

Theatre of the Oppressed (TO) was first developed by Augusto Boal with a central purpose to combat oppression (Sullivan et al., 2008) by eliciting audience participation in each and all variations and expressions of TO aesthetics and dramatic/performance approaches (Fantus, 2020; Garcia, Crifasi & Dessel, 2019; Wynne, 2019). As alluded to above, in TO, the audience is encouraged to move from a more traditional, passive consumption of drama by engaging in the development of in-the-moment aesthetics and outcomes of TO (Santos, 2016). Specifically, in TO, audience members are asked to actively engage in drama and performance by intervening during TO preformances by providing suggestions on plot development, which involves improvisation from actors. Interventions come by way of audiences providing realistic conflict resolutions that reflect the socioeconomic and political conditions they face in their lives. Sometimes, audience participation occurs when they arrive in the TO space and after the formal performance when critical dialogues continue. In summary, real-time interventions (e.g., altering the plot) are aimed at alleviating oppression and empowering oppressed audience members to find solutions for problems they may be facing in their lives and communities.

TO has been described as a powerful vehicle for the development of critical reflection and consciousness (van Bewer et al., 2021). The aims of TO can be found throughout Boal's writing and in the literature that I have been referencing. Based on this literature and my personal experience with TO and its many approaches, I support the idea that the key difference between TO and other forms of dramatization (e.g., method acting) is TO's core principles encouraging actors to develop a deep knowledge of one's own body and to use the body and drama/performance as a language that can convey specific messages about liberation (Giesler, 2017). In so doing, the performer/actor can help to build what I see as dramatic and thrilling spaces to encourage not silence and quiet conduct but active dialogue among audience members before, during, and after the performance.

Using various methods, active interaction empowers individuals who share similar social identities to collectively "rehearse" the actions they may decide to enact in real-world situations (Corsa, 2020; Fantus, 2020; Garcia et al., 2019; Wynne, 2019). TO interactions can include physical games, image-making exercises, character creation, scene-building, and plot improvisations (Sullivan et al., 2008). The example in the box below exemplifies the basic format of TO, which has been described in the extant global literature. That literature shows that TO audiences have aptly identified conflicts and provided real-time pragmatic solutions to myriad dramatized forms of oppression and prejudices (Giesler, 2017; van Bewer et al., 2021), such as those highlighted in Chapter 1.

> **Example of TO in Action.** Sydney, Australia: TO is used to address questions concerning power and resistance around uneven balance of power between a large public housing estate and real estate developers (Wynne, 2019). In the first scene, residents begin to engage with one another as they find out that real estate profiteers intend to "redevelop" the area where they live. The second scene centers around residents in conversation with a community development worker who is providing information on the redevelopment plans. The worker is unable to answer the residents' questions. In the third scene, the government attempts to coerce residents into accepting the terms of redevelopment. In the final scene, which is more contemplative, residents receive letters about their relocation. These scenes are revisited in the second act where the "Curinga" (Joker, in English) pauses the performance and encourages the audience to speculate different outcomes to the issues explored in the first act.

This same literature, considered above, suggests that poorly executed, TO may not achieve the level of engagement that would evoke reflection and action. A common critique of TO is its focus on individual-level outcomes in the form of reflection and action and a lack of evidence that TO can realistically affect structural changes in larger systems of oppression (Baer, Salisbury, & Goldstein, 2019). As suggested by Wynne (2019), placing the main outcomes of TO on the individual may inadvertently place the responsibility of combating oppression on under-resourced people with marginalized identities. Furthermore, there is concern that a safe space may not always be available to enact TO techniques, and facilitators may lack the necessary, proper training to implement the different approaches within TO (Fantus, 2020; Geisler, 2017). Nonetheless, TO has expanded beyond Brazil and has been shown to be useful globally using various approaches discussed below.

Theater of the Oppressed Approaches & Their Applications

This book is not intended to be an extensive study of the approaches/techniques that have made TO a widespread method for helping people engage in social discourse and action. However, here, I provide a brief overview of key approaches, which can be combined with and modified alongside other theatrical approaches, such as method acting. Of particular interest is solo performance, which is the approach I used in *Marília*.

Theater of the Oppressed Approaches. Based on its core principles and sensibilities, six different types/techniques/ approaches have grown from *Theatre of the Oppressed*. These are: (1) Forum Theater; (2) Legislative Theater; (3) Image Theater; (4) Invisible Theater; (5) Newspaper Theater; and (6) Rainbow of Desire. Each of these approaches encourages audience and community engagement to facilitate dialogues, reflection, and action against myriad forms of oppression.

Forum Theater is the most well-known and widely used form of TO. Its main approach involves small groups of individuals performing scenes aimed to depict day-to-day living in communities whose members face myriad forms of oppression and prejudice. Here the audience interacts and suggests strategies to encourage action and conflict mitigation. The questions I pose (examples below) in the text and performances of *Marília* evoke the forum approach in that audience members were given time to briefly discuss their thoughts about my questions that were meant to confront prejudice and stereotypes and then discuss different outcomes. The three passages below are not specific examples of TO approaches. I provide them here to show three examples of how we can live up to core TO principles even when using different dramatic methods—in this case, self-referential theater in solo performance.

> PROTAGONIST: "The same straight boys who mocked me also chased me around as though I was a girl ... I was confused by all this. Even more confused when adults asked me, 'Are you a boy or a girl?' I was asked often, 'Are you a boy or a girl,' even after I became a teenager."

> PROTAGONIST: "I feel so heavy ... heavy and old ... old and fat! Do I look fat? Growing up I was so skinny, a scrawny kid! There was never enough food. My mother worked hard all day to feed all of us ... "

> PROTAGONIST: "Deep down, I thought that I'd see you intact in your coffin, untouched by men, free of obsession, inside the earth as if nothing ever happened. I desperately wanted to finally find *myself* looking pretty like you, but what did I find? Nothing! Bits and pieces! Who are you, little sister, lovely images or rotten fragments? I am so angry that no one was there to save you from that fucking bus. Where was everybody? Where?"

Newspaper Theater can be used to turn a piece of daily news into a more dramatic and useful information. Individual performers can recite a new item of news while also adding new information that was omitted from the original news piece. *Image Theater* usually involves one performer interacting with one or more audience members to use their bodies to develop/sculpt interactive forms to tell a story and/or enact a conflict. My use of projections in my performances of *Marília* communicates with this form of TO in that I used text as I "sculpted" images to create conflict. For example, when I recite an entire poem, *Oh! My father ...,* about my father's molestation of me when I was a child, while his image is shown behind me on a screen.

Legislative Theater is used to inform audience members about the laws that often exacerbate their oppressed lives—e.g., laws that promote the incarceration of humans. In this approach, actors often perform the roles of policymakers who elicit help in creating legislative bills that aim to protect individuals and communities against discrimination and oppression. *Invisible Theater* often employs improvisation in public settings to convey naturally occurring events. By using current events as the main script, Invisible Theater aims to raise awareness about current social or political issues. *Rainbow of Desire* is a technique used to explore interpersonal connections and the conflicts that may arise out of them.

All these approaches can be used individually or grouped to achieve greater effect. The various approaches in the TO can stand alone in their potential to evoke critical dialogue and reflection, and even action, beyond the performance, by audience members. Furthermore, the literature shows that TO has been used alongside other theatrical and dramatic methods to enhance the goals and outcomes of a performance, as exemplified with scenes from *Marília*, above.

Now that I have established the basic concepts of TO and its theoretical and practical relationship to the pedagogy of the oppressed, and following the central aim of this book, in Chapter 3, I will further demonstrate the usefulness of drama and performance vis-à-vis the issues highlighted in my play *Marília*, focusing specifically on how to spark critical dialogues with the potential to help audiences engage in reflection and action toward liberation.

3

Biographical Drama and Performance for Self-Healing and Liberation

In this chapter, I describe and explain the usefulness of self-referential theater, also referred to here as autobiographical drama and solo performance as vehicles for self-healing and social liberation.

Self-Referential Theater or Autobiographical Drama is often used in solo performances—a one-person show featuring a single person telling a story for an audience. It has been suggested that the purpose of solo performance that uses biographical material is to entertain, of course, but also to allow the performer to pursue self-healing by sharing intimate details about one's life (Emunah, 2015; Heddon, 2008). The performer tacitly encourages the audience to engage in self-healing, a process of self-analysis, akin to the process used by the performer who uses autobiographical material. This process involves gentle confrontation of past psychological conflicts steered by one's own motivation and inspired by the performance. This approach connects to the

Theatre of the Oppressed principle of audience participation as it creates opportunities for self-healing by way of a cooperative process (Kohrt et al., 2020) of empathizing with the performer and with one another.

Self-referential material is the essence of *Pedagogy of the Oppressed* as it represents a human being's existence based on that individual's take on their life experiences, perceptions, feelings, attitudes, opinions, certainties, and doubts. Similarly, performance based on authentic self-referential material is the essence of *Theatre of the Oppressed* (TO), as self-referential material has the potential to create inspiring drama and conflict when audiences can see parts of themselves in those engaged in solo performances. Using self-referential material, solo performers invite their audiences to develop a sense of acquaintance with them and other audience members. Such an acquaintance often encourages audience members to empathize with the performer's plight and to imagine that other people in the audience who live under similar socioeconomic and political circumstances may be sharing similar thoughts and feelings regarding the issues highlighted in the performance in real time.

Personal and Social Power in Solo Performance

One-person plays, also known as solo performances, are a powerful form of theater where a single actor shares a personal story. These are often intimate performances aimed at creating a deep connection between the performer and their audience and making the audience an integral part of the dramatic experience. Unlike traditional theater, which involves more than one performer and can be experienced as more distant to the audience, one-person plays draw audience members through direct engagement, such as in direct eye contact and by asking the audience questions that encourage an internal dialogue. A key aspect of a one-person play is its ability to convey the voice of marginalized communities through the voice of a performer who shares similar marginalization.

One-person plays, often performed in small theaters or public spaces, can also provide an affordable alternative for artists, allowing them to tell their stories without the need for large budgets or complex productions that include numerous performers. Solo performances focus on universal themes like love, loss, and resilience, giving marginalized voices a platform to be heard. Sharing similar principles as TO, solo performances aim to create emotional connections derived from autobiographical content from real people, to help audiences feel more empathetic, build understanding around the performer's social identities, and thus encourage reflection concerning the circumstances of their own lives. In my view, an impactful one-person play leaves lasting cognitive and emotional impressions, fosters deeper connections between performer and audience members, and makes personal stories accessible to all.

For example, one-person plays whose contents focus on Black/African American histories and cultures have inspired and uplifted audiences holding Black/African American backgrounds and others with myriad racial/ethnic identities. Often rooted in African storytelling traditions and shaped by the resilience of enslaved people's narratives, solo performances originating from the struggles of individuals and their communities embody the spirit of empowerment and self-expression. Being less costly than full-cast productions and thus easier to produce, solo plays provide a creative outlet for Black artists (and other marginalized groups) who have often faced barriers to accessing mainstream theater opportunities. As Vacca (1997) suggests, people with myriad oppressed social identities, such as Black women, have performed their poetry, prose, and dramas outside of theaters in churches, clubs, and lodges, many of which became central to the development of Black theater in America. By choosing intimate spaces and performances, minoritized artists have showcased their talent as they shared deeply personal stories that resonate with their struggles, joys, and triumphs of Black communities, continuing a legacy of resilience and artistry.

Solo performance has the power to create a personal, intimate connection that pulls the audience into the story being told by a friendly performer. The direct engagement initiated by the performer helps audience members to feel deeply involved, as the performer speaks directly to them, often asking questions and/or sharing confessions—e.g., *The Bookshop*, where Rose, the storyteller, reflects on her life, her love for books, and the struggles she faced (Siberz, 2009). As she shares her story, the audience is invited to join her in her journey. Her decision to close the shop is deeply tied to the changing socioeconomic world around her—big bookstores, discount retailers like Costco, and exploitive online stores like Amazon that have made it impossible for small bookshops to survive. This direct engagement encourages viewers to see the world through Rose's eyes, fostering a deeper understanding of the challenges she faces. By immersing themselves in the story, audience members can reflect on the personal struggles of Rose and others living in similar circumstances and then take action to change what is happening around them.

For another example of how a solo performance can be intimate and impactful in revealing the experiences of a marginalized person and their communities, Shain's (2005) analysis highlights how solo performances can empower people with disabilities to take control of their own narratives, challenge stereotypes, and promote inclusivity. Shain's performances are designed to make the audience relate to him as a person and not solely to his disability. Often, disabled people are portrayed in ways that emphasize their needs and challenges performing daily tasks that are made difficult by the lack of universal designs that would help them to function like other non-disabled people. This type of theater often isolates many different facets of the humanity of people with disabilities. Shain demonstrates the power of solo performance by focusing on universal human characteristics such as desires, love, need for connection and purpose, and aspects of life shared by *all* human beings.

Autobiographical Drama and *Theatre of the Oppressed*

It is not my goal to draw a direct theoretical connection between the above examples and *Theatre of the Oppressed*. I am, however, trying to show how solo performances by and about marginalized people evoke key principles of TO in that it aims, as does TO, to help audience members with similar social identities to imagine key aspects of their lives performed on stage or another type of venue. Solo performance, by focusing on universal issues shared by all human beings, can also create the emotional closeness needed for people whose life experiences may dramatically differ from those of the performer to imagine and reflect on what it might be to live the life of the performer. Perhaps the main connection here is with concepts of popular education (Portuguese, *educação popular*), advanced by Freire, who saw adult education as something that needed to bring about not only specific subject matters but, perhaps most importantly, the integration and encouragement of critical reflection in all activities concerning "education," all aimed at improving critical consciousness and advance social liberation (Haddad & Di Pierro, 2021). This notion is reflected in *Marília*, for example, as I, the solo performer, use visual cues as didactic techniques to "teach" an adult audience of mostly Americans, often unfamiliar with Brazilian history, the realities of a dictatorship and the poverty it fosters while inviting audience members to empathize (critical reflection) with the plight of immigrants to the United States. This is exemplified in the passages of *Marília* below.

> **PROTAGONIST:** "I came from a housing project in Belo Horizonte. [*Projection: Housing Project*] There, we played barefoot on the dirt, grass, and unpaved streets [*Projection: Housing Project grounds*] … Marília's accident took place at the bus stop in front of that building. [*Projection grounds# 12 fades*] From the building's open courtyard, we could see inside each apartment. We knew one another's intimate business. The police often raided the buildings without any apparent reason. Growing up under the dictatorship, lack of privacy was commonplace."

> **PROTAGONIST:** "The pace of the city and the cold weather pushed me to eat more, dare more, try new things. I even considered becoming a whore; some immigrants do. We look for warmth in strangers who may help us with money, sometimes food. I didn't have it in me to become a whore, but I wonder … if I had a pussy and long straight hair … would I have?"

In conveying real-life experiences while questioning the status quo, solo performers are, in fact, establishing a critical dialogue with their audiences. In my own experience performing both *Marília* and its adaptation *Realm of the Dead*, described in previous chapters, even in the deepest moments of silence, such dialogue was palpable and then confirmed by numerous audience members who, voluntarily or through evaluation tools, shared their experiences of the performance. Audiences often shared with me that critical reflections about myriad conflicts unearthed by the dramatic materials I presented continued after the performance, as their testimonials below exemplify.

> Thank you for …. your deeply moving work of art … I'm inspired to think about how we can carry the energy from your work forward.
>
> It was very emotional; I was not exactly sure what it was until attending, and I was pleasantly surprised. I tried putting myself in the shoes of the performer, and it was heartbreaking for me to even imagine losing a sister.
>
> I had a great experience … It made me think about the complexity of humankind and how people are able to perceive themselves and shape other people's perceptions of them through art and storytelling.

Having previously established key connections between Freire's *Pedagogy of the Oppressed* and Boal's TO, I now turn to the literature suggesting that combining different forms of drama and performance does not conflict or detract from the key tenets of TO. In fact, by reinventing some of its key approaches or combining them might potentiate the main desired impacts of critical reflection and action. For example, Fox and Leeder (2015) demonstrate how playback and self-referential theater (autobiographical drama) can be used together to amplify the voices of those trying to combat injustice. Self-referential theater can be used with playback theater for onstage storytelling, followed by the performer eliciting audience members to reenact portions of the story they just told. Here again, a major goal of TO is being achieved as playback theater is used to provide audience members an opportunity to reenact and witness life stories with which they can relate and thus empathize. For specific examples of the exploration of cross-cultural interactions, social identities, and myriad social justice themes, I recommend reading Fox and Leeder's (2015) book. Similar to my approach in *Marília*, here, the authors emphasize layered approaches to drama and performance. In *Marília*, I use auto*ethno*graphic content in what I have come to understand to be an excellent choice for autobiographical solo drama and performance.

Auto*ethno*graphic Drama and Performance frequently contains autobiographical content—personal aspects of one's life—plus a focus on auto*ethno*graphic material that may include myriad positionalities, or social identities, such as one's race, ethnicity, gender, sexual orientation, primary and secondary languages, and others. Auto*ethno*graphic material may also include socioeconomic and political conditions, such as poverty status, political affiliation, social class, marginalized work status (e.g., unemployed, sex work), immigration status (e.g., undocumented), and other personal and/or social characteristics.

Traditional media often portrays marginalized people by focusing almost exclusively on the aspects of their lives that made them marginalized—i.e., their social identities and the socioeconomic and political conditions around which they live. Auto*ethno*graphic drama and performance often challenge systemic barriers and prejudices by highlighting that society— not the performer—creates and maintains these barriers and prejudices. In so doing, auto*ethno*graphic drama and performance promote a shared experience between performers and audiences in which their emotions and identities blend together in the form of empathy for one another; the audience not only watches but also actively participates in the storytelling. This sets the solo performance of auto*ethno*graphic content apart from traditional theater. While traditional theater can evoke strong emotions, the personal connection in one-person plays is often more immediate and profound, and it thus facilitates the audience to experience a deeper connection to the story.

Autobiographical Drama and Self-Healing

In "Why We Heal: The Evolution of Psychological Healing and Implications for Global Mental Health," Kohrt et al. (2020) pose the question, "Why do humans heal one another?" Myriad disciplines, including evolutionary psychology, social work, sociology, and psychiatry, have provided evidence for how and why human beings suffer from and are confronted with psychosocial distress, whose intensity can be explained by how the socioeconomic and political environment interact with/influence the manifestation of human beings' genetic materials. History shows that people with marginalized identities have been oppressed by the ruling classes and thus have been disparately affected by historical trauma and mental illness. Kohrt et al. use evolutionary theory to explain why human beings naturally wish to engage in the process of psychologically supporting one another. I wish to make a connection between this assertion and both the goals of TO and autobiographical drama.

TO and autobiographical drama provide the basis for a solo performer to share with their audiences the details of their histories of oppression while disclosing their daily emotions which they need to regulate interpersonally. Regulation of emotions—how we show our authentic selves and receive input from others—is the key to how human beings can soothe and help to heal one another from psychosocial distress. A solo performer that uses auto*ethno*graphic material has the power to create an opportunity for the performer and their audiences to engage in psychosocial healing by way of what Kohrt and colleagues identified as a process of cooperation and emotional contagion. Autobiographical drama also provides an opportunity to explore social contexts (e.g., autocratic regimes) in which social and political oppression obstructs human beings' ability to empathize and console each other out of fear of retribution.

In *Marília,* I confront myriad positionalities (race, ethnicity, immigrant status) and the social oppression that existed in my past and persists in the present. They include xenophobia, racism, and homophobia. As discussed in Chapter 1, those of us who must deal with these oppressions daily are more likely to develop oppression-related symptoms manifested as emotional depression and anxiety. Therefore, autobiographical drama has been used for therapeutic purposes, including better understanding oneself, solving emotional problems, and holistic self-healing. The literature suggests that the exploration of auto*ethno*graphic content through playwriting and solo performance has been used to address traumatic life events, substance misuse sequelae, and mental health difficulties (Heddon, 2008). In Chapter 4, I will provide theoretical and empirical evidence for integrating arts-based interventions to abate unwarranted psychological, physiological, social, and behavioral issues.

In my play *Marília,* I aimed to work out important issues in my personal life by telling the story of the loss of my sister and the vacuum that such loss created for my entire family. However, the story is told while emphasizing the deplorable socioeconomic conditions created by a military coup followed by a twenty-one-year dictatorship. In *Marília,* I am working out a cluster of traumatic events—the main one being the tragic death of my sister and my parsing out the details of how she died and who to blame for her demise. In *Marília,* I used the common technique of becoming another character that is integral to the plot but who is performed by a solo performer. To parse out blame and to fully reveal the many narratives of *how* my sister died, I performed the unique narrative of each of my sisters and my mother by becoming each of them. For each, I created monologues that allowed me to explore their conflicting doubts, guilt, sorrow, and sadness and then enact them on stage. The lines below exemplify these ideas from the monologue I used to portray my mother. The following quoted text comprises the lines that I recited as myself to explain to my audiences how I had integrated my sisters and my mother into my psyche.

> **PROTAGONIST (AS MOTHER):** "All I know is that early in the day Marília died, she smeared lipstick all over herself, Rogério, and the pet rabbit. I asked my older daughters to clean them up and watch them while I went downtown to run some errands … before I left, I promised Marília that I'd bring cookies for her … I came back a couple of hours later: Marília saw me on the bus and ran outside to greet me … The driver didn't see her! Suddenly, there she was, my daughter, lying on the pavement … We buried her the next day. My baby looked like an angel … This is all I can remember, but Suzana, my oldest daughter, should know more, she was supposed to watch Marília."

> **PROTAGONIST:** "This has been true all my life; my mother and sisters have … given me so much I could never list it all … Pink lipstick, light and delicate like Marília … a little mirror reflecting both our faces … little things that make us both happy. Without my mother and all my sisters, I would not be here today. I am at once each and all of them."

I believe that self-healing can be achieved when a performer transforms personal conflict into storytelling to an audience that is primed to cooperate in mutual contagion, and to personal self-healing goals, advance artistic, educational, and advocacy efforts. After I had performed *Marília* several times in 2022, I stated that "*Marília* was written as a play because I felt that the story needed to be experienced live (not told), with audience participation" (Pinto, 2022c). From the time I began to write *Marília*, I felt an existential need to delve more deeply into my life and to write more auto*ethno*graphic material for solo and ensemble performances. My approach has been akin to a confession that embraces my life's raw realities and myriad interpretations. The goal for me is to deconstruct fake realities, embrace my sense of power and vulnerability, and ultimately understand and share my multifaceted identities with my audiences (Adams & Holman-Jones, 2011).

As an academic and a practicing artist, I have used auto-*ethno*graphic playwriting and performance for investigational pursuits and experimentation. I agree with others that the outcomes of what we do are important, and they do need validation from us and our audiences; however, my focus is more on the process of writing and performing than on the actual outcomes (Emunah, 2020). This connects back to Boal's *Theatre of the Oppressed* in that the end of a play or an exercise can be changed as the audience is invited to intervene in the plot and aesthetics of a performance. This allows for both improvisation and experimentation, also known as "self-revelatory performance," which encourages solo performers to engage in deep exploration of how they develop a relationship with their audience before, during, and after a performance (Emunah, 2015; Emunah, 2020).

It is important to note that self-referential theater does not always include storytelling and dramatization of real-life events and experiences aimed at pursuing self-healing (Emunah, 2015). Autobiographical material can also be used for purposes other than therapeutic ones, such as art-based education, advocacy, and activism. Regardless of its main purpose, whether therapeutic or not, autobiographical and auto*ethno*graphic material is often used to improve our understanding of how all our social identities evolve inconsistently and ambiguously over time (Anthias, 2008). For example, in *Marília*, the protagonist, a cisgender-appearing gay man, tries to work out issues concerning the sequelae of sexual molestation by questioning his gender identities while suggesting his fleeting desire to have female genitalia.

PROTAGONIST: "As a child, I thought what made a girl a girl was having a pussy. All my sisters had pussies. If I had one, I'd be just like Marília, right? A Marília who never died. In my mind, everyone thought I might be a girl. I knew I was a girl, even though I didn't have a pussy. I began to wonder if my father also knew I was a girl … the way he looked at me … showed special interest in me … I was confused … you see, my father touched me intimately. His touch was firm, manly; he was a man. Therefore, I must be a "girl.""

In the process of writing *Marília*, I had lengthy conversations with my mother before she passed away in 2012. I was unable to talk to my father because he died when I was still a child. I also talked to my six siblings, who are all still alive. Though the text of *Marília* does include my two brothers, they have been integral parts of my pursuit to understand how Marília died. In my investigational pursuit, all my siblings and my mother have helped me with the socioeconomic and political context around the events that led to my sister's demise. They are witnesses without whose testimonies I could not put together the puzzle that troubled me my entire life. In this sense, I began to heal long before I started to write the play. By talking to my family and friends of the family, who also witnessed our plight, I experienced cooperation and emotional contagion that facilitated self-healing and a better understanding of my internal conflicts. I experienced cooperation and emotional contagion again during and after every performance of *Marília* and its adaptation, *Realm of the Dead*.

The last scene in Marília sums up for me what can be accomplished by using autobiographical material in a solo performance in terms of self-healing that can be shared numerous times directly with audiences. In the last scene, the protagonist holds Marília, represented by a life-size doll, and recites to her a poem, "Marília's lullaby," which evokes the protagonist's sense of healing as he feels emotionally

FIGURE 3.1 *Marília's Lullaby*
Photo by Nikki Williams depicting the protagonist on stage holding Marília as he prepares to place her in a coffin.

strong enough to let his sister rest in peace. Throughout the play, Marília is displayed as if she had never left or as if the protagonist never let her leave. After the protagonist recites the poem, he places his sister back in her coffin and closes it as he says the following words.

> **PROTAGONIST:** "You deserve to rest … Sweet sister, Marília … Go, go to heaven … On earth no more."

4

Drama and Performance to Cultivate Empathy and Well-Being

In this chapter, I reflect on issues I presented in previous chapters, delving into connections between oppression and well-being and empathy as they relate to a conceptual framework, the *Minority Stress Model*.

Well-Being. "Well-being" is often used to mean good health, joy, happiness, life satisfaction, or any combination of these. Well-being can act as a buffer against stress. It can help people improve their capacities to manage their thoughts and feelings, their sense of meaning and purpose, and their social connections (Centers for Disease Control and Prevention, 2024).

Empathy. African American author Isabel Wilkerson (*Caste, the Warmth of Other Suns*) defines "radical empathy" as a person's work toward educating themself and listening to others' life experiences from their perspectives. The anticipated result is a human connection that allows one person to understand how another perceives their own joys and pains (Wilkerson, 2020).

Here, I use Tan et al.'s *Minority Stress Model*, which has been used multiple times to suggest how day-to-day forms of oppression (e.g., racial discrimination, homophobia) cause myriad negative health and mental health outcomes for those already having marginalized and minoritized social identities. I also summarize research indicating that art forms, particularly drama and performance (D&P), have been used to cultivate empathy or well-being. Definitions of well-being and empathy abound in the literature; nonetheless, there are no better definitions than those we establish for ourselves within the parameters of our lives. This way we embrace the best types of well-being or empathy *for us* and how to pursue it *them*. The pursuit of well-being and empathy, and the connections we make between the two, are felt at a personal level. Our personal definitions of these human experiences may change over time. Therefore, in this book, I use the terms "well-being" and "empathy" as defined above.

The *Minority Stress Model* focuses our attention on myriad life stressors (Ramirez & Paz-Galupo, 2019) as follows. Distal stressors include environmental forces, such as violence and harassment, against marginalized and minoritized people. Proximal stressors refer to internalized oppression, the impact of prejudicial treatment, which includes the fear of being discriminated. This is most evident when a person feels threatened to the point of concealing their identity, for example, by hiding one's sexual orientation. Unlike one-time life stressors, for example, the loss of a loved one or having a heart attack, minority stress is conceptualized as being long-lasting and pervasive as it comes from constant exposure to socioeconomic and political oppression and prejudice. Those stressors are thus associated with prolonged psychosocial and emotional strain.

Minority Stress Model. This model describes how socio-economic and political stressors targeting marginalized people can contribute to negative life outcomes. It suggests that the cumulative impact of oppression in its myriad forms can, over time, induce and/or exacerbate physical and psychological issues. The result of oppression, the ongoing experience of stigma and prejudice, often lead to stress/distress. This psychosocial framework can help us understand the mental and physical health challenges experienced by individuals with social identities—e.g., people of color, transgender, gay, people with disabilities—that have been historically stigmatized and marginalized (Flentje et al., 2020; Frost & Meyer, 2023; Hoy-Ellis, 2023).

As examples, using the *Minority Stress Model* as a theoretical framework, Tan et al. (2020) studied stressors specific to trans and gender-diverse people compared to cisgender people. The authors found that issues such as negative social expectations (distal stressors) and internalized transphobia (proximal stressors) contribute to increased experiences of stress and lack of well-being. As previously discussed, racial discrimination is closely tied to heightened stress levels, often resulting from being the recipient of daily social, economic, and political aggression and violence. This type of stress has been shown to influence negative health outcomes (e.g., cigarette smoking, high blood pressure, and cardiovascular problems) and to undermine social outcomes such as well-being, lack of trust, and reduced social interaction (Brondolo et al., 2012; Harrell, 2000).

Arts-Based Psychosocial Interventions

More research is needed to demonstrate further the longitudinal impact of prejudice and oppression in different groups of marginalized and minoritized humans. Nonetheless, the extant literature explored below shows the empirical evidence and, thus, the potential for using arts-based psychosocial interventions to abate adverse outcomes stemming from oppression, which include the abuse and lack of care people with minoritized and marginalized identities are exposed every day.

Arts-based Intervention. Among the many definitions of "arts-based intervention," I have learned that they can be understood as informal or formalized activities, or combinations of activities, in which art forms or art media are used by individuals or groups to improve their lives and overall well-being by ameliorating their emotional, psychological, and physical health. Arts-based interventions may include one or more art forms, such as visual art—painting, drawing, sculpture, etc., prose and poetry, culinary arts, craft-making, and the performing arts—music, drama, dance, poetry— among others.

In 2019, the World Health Organization published a scoping review of over 3,000 studies showing that being exposed to different art forms has the potential to promote health and well-being at the individual and environmental levels (Fancourt & Finn, 2019). More specifically, among their many benefits, arts-based interventions have been shown to influence emotional and psychological well-being, self-healing, social interaction and interpersonal communication, self-esteem, and social skills. The extant literature indicates that arts-based interventions have had different types of impact on myriad populations. As examples, in the past couple of years alone, arts-based interventions and art therapies have been used successfully to promote health in migrant populations (Oepen & Gruber, 2024), quality of life in cancer patients (Ünal & Yüce, 2025), wellness among indigenous people

(Motta-Ochoa et al., 2024), stress relief in college students (Liu et al., 2024), and to foster creativity in diverse workforces (Bacouël et al., 2024). The benefits of arts-based interventions have inspired researchers, practitioners, and the public, as they have been shown to cultivate social engagement and empathy among community members and, thus, greater well-being.

Theatre of the Oppressed as a Psychosocial Intervention

The extant literature contains numerous publications describing and explaining how TO approaches have been impactful in cultivating social justice and well-being. It is worth noting a few examples of how TO can be used with diverse populations in different spaces to achieve different outcomes that ultimately generate well-being among those receiving the intervention and/or those who, through social contagion (see Chapter 3), may also benefit from the intervention; for example, patients of medical care professionals trained by receiving arts-based interventions. I am discussing those TO-related interventions here to establish the foundation for why I believe solo drama and performance (D&P) have great potential to help us cultivate empathy and well-being. This is presented separately below.

TO has also been studied for its utility in creating a safe space in the classroom. Described as a new type of learning method, TO has been used, for example, to prompt students to create sculptures and stories on a designated marginalized group, e.g., the LGBTQIA2+ community, aimed to help people develop insight into the struggles faced by these groups (Garcia, Crifasi, & Dessel, 2019). Also using TO's legislative approach, Saeed (2015) studied an intervention that can empower women in places overwhelmed by war, conflict, and human abuse, in this case, Afghanistan. Furthermore, TO has been widely used and studied within medical spaces where it has been used for capacity building, for engaging patients in their own recovery, and for improving patient well-being. Since the focus of this chapter, and this book in general, is on well-being, I provide other examples related to issues concerning well-being in different groups below.

TO has been used to a great degree of success to engage medical students to embrace ethical behaviors and to advance health equity (Chin et al., 2023). In the form of forum theater, TO has been shown to promote interdisciplinary teamwork in healthcare settings by encouraging nurses to engage in reflective practice and person-centered care (van Bewer et al., 2021). These studies exemplify the major pursuit of social justice goals by helping health professionals center their practices on the specific needs of marginalized and minoritized populations. Professionals participating in those studies were encouraged to reflect on their roles as health providers critically and then act toward the betterment of their patients (critical action). As a reminder, this is the meaning behind the concept of critical consciousness, the process that encompasses critical reflection and action discussed in previous chapters.

TO has been used to help prevent sexism and sexual harassment (Lüthi et al., 2022). In this study, the authors described an intervention not unlike my play *Marília*, which includes interactions and the use of both images and drama. By using these techniques, those involved learned new strategies and approaches for addressing sexism and sexual harassment in medical schools. A study in South Africa shows that mental health in maternity wards can be improved by exposing women to forum theater (Honikman, Field, & Cooper, 2019). To abate patient abuse, the authors created performances aimed at developing empathy among nurses caring for pregnant women. Other key goals included helping participants to improve awareness of their thoughts and feelings (critical reflection) and actions toward their patients.

In all the examples above, by following key principles of TO audience interaction and using different TO approaches, in each of these cases, audience members were encouraged to engage with the script and help performers reimagine different scenarios and conflict resolutions. These and most examples in the extant literature demonstrate a deep level of care about helping both audience members and performers develop and improve empathy for one another and to use that empathy to accept and celebrate their different social identities and the different types of oppression they face in their lives. In all TO approaches found in the literature, whether TO is used in social or professional settings, I have come to understand that the main benefit of TO is that it brings performers and audiences together to engage in psychosocial healing through the process of cooperation and emotional contagion that I described in Chapter 3. This process can improve human beings' capacity not only to empathize but to console each other (Kohrt et al., 2020). This type of social support, in turn, helps people engage in critical reflection and action.

Drama and Performance as a Psychosocial Intervention

As the evidence shows above, TO, an art-based intervention, substantiates my assertion that art forms in general, and specifically theater and solo drama and performance (D&P), can help address systemic oppression and prejudice, improve empathy among humans, and achieve specific outcomes, such as better health, mental health, and well-being. I believe this is possible because engagement with the performing arts—live music, theater performance—has been empirically linked with improved social connectedness and the outcomes outlined throughout this book; for example, see Perkins et al. (2021).

Figure 4.1 provides a visual representation, in the format of a diagram, of how I see D&P as potential vehicles for the process of cooperation and emotional contagion, critical

Drama & Performance Improve Well-Being

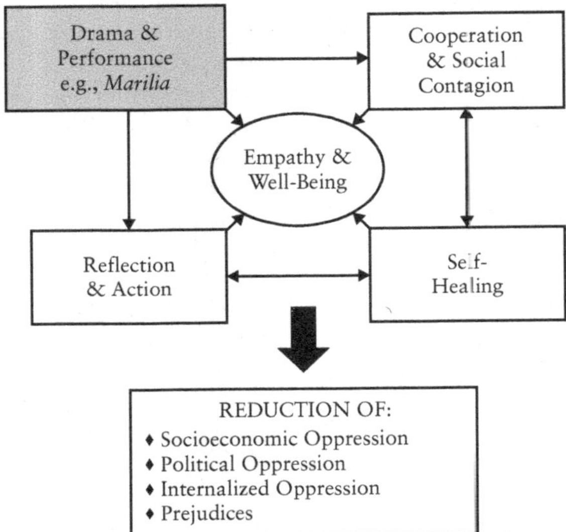

FIGURE 4.1 *Drama and performance improve empathy and well-being.*

reflection and action, and self-healing, as I have described thus far. This process applies to how I see my solo performance of *Marília* as an art intervention that follows the contours of the diagram below.

The bottom portion of the diagram represents the socioeconomic and political oppressions and prejudices faced by marginalized and minoritized groups and the pernicious effect of oppression when it is internalized by members of those groups. In the top portion of the diagram, the double-headed arrows indicate interactions between and across the different variables that can help us cultivate empathy and well-being. The diagram shows how D&P (e.g., *Marília*) can promote both critical reflection and action, as well as cooperation and social contagion among performers and audience members.

These, in turn, and interactively, promote self-healing. The circle in the middle represents the key outcomes of arts-based interventions, namely, well-being and empathy. The diagram indicates that well-being and empathy are outcomes of D&P written and staged for meaningful audience interaction, as defined by Boal and as I have discussed throughout this book. The small arrows pointing at "Empathy & Well-Being" indicate that both are influenced by *all* elements of the diagram.

D&P Cultivate Empathy and Well-Being

The extant literature showing how D&P can influence empathy and well-being is mostly descriptive and explanatory. In other words, the evidence comes from personal narratives, anecdotes, and numerous papers describing and explaining the effects of D&P. Predictive studies, particularly experimental and semi-experimental ones, would help improve what we know about the impact of arts-based interventions. However, putting together the vast information from across the globe, I am confident that D&P continue to have enormous potential to combat oppression and prejudice, as initially revealed by the work of both Freire and Boal. In this context, D&P refer to theatrical performative drama. All the examples I have used thus far fit this description, including my play *Marília*, which is an autobiographical drama that I have performed several times.

Far from being only entertainment, D&P are vehicles for creativity and self-discovery. D&P afford people various ways to express their opinions and emotions, confront the socioeconomic and political challenges they face in their lives, and build empathy and well-being in ways that feel most natural and engaging. Freire and Boal used myriad different forms of art in their work because they realized that art, in this specific case D&P, speaks to the core of what makes us human, which is, in essence, our need to connect, to understand ourselves, and to feel understood. Below, I discuss several ways that different approaches to D&P have been used to help people cultivate empathy for one another and to improve their own well-being. Here, I organized key pieces of evidence for using D&P as an intervention to cultivate both empathy and well-being—key ingredients for critical reflection and action.

Improvisational theater, or "improv," is a spontaneous form of performance where performers create dialogue, characters, and scenes mainly without a script. However, even in improv, performers often develop outlines for their performances, keeping in mind that their audiences will react and participate in ways that may, in turn, influence the sequence and outcomes within each of their performances. In so doing, they create moments of empathy, which can occur in any type of solo performance, even those fully scripted, such as the case of *Marília*. Openness to changing one's performance underscores the values of collaboration and adaptability, also present in TO, making it a powerful tool for personal growth and emotional resilience.

Research highlights improv's potential to enhance creativity and well-being by fostering critical thinking and behavioral changes. Research suggests that improv participants experience improved self-esteem, self-efficacy, and resilience (Schwenke et al., 2020). For example, among older adults, participation in improv improved personal growth, relationships, self-esteem, and overall well-being while reducing depressive symptoms. These benefits persist for months post-intervention (Keisari et al., 2020). Similarly, improv-based training for young people vulnerable to psychotic symptoms has been shown to alleviate hallucinations, delusions, and social withdrawal (Tang et al., 2020). Psychodrama, another strategy explored below, has also been shown to help adolescents and young adults cope with cancer by promoting well-being (Testoni et al., 2020).

Psychodrama is an impactful strategy for healing and growth. It allows participants to reenact past experiences, address current conflicts, and/or envision the future they desire. For instance, Autobiographical Therapeutic Performance (ATP)—a form of psychodrama—has been shown to improve executive functioning in adults affected by trauma, mental health challenges, and environmental problems, such as involvement in legal systems (see, for example, Ray & Pendzik, 2021). For this study, participants worked with theater coaches to create performances based on autobiographical material, storytelling, and improvisation. The material produced by participants was later used in a theatrical production performed by professional actors. ATP participants reported improvements in interpersonal relationships. The extant literature suggests that everyone, whether they are less or more active in D&P, can contribute toward the process of cultivating empathy and well-being. As suggested by Figure 4.1, the concept of cooperation and social contagion was reflected in Giacomucci and Marquit's (2020) research on trauma-focused psychodrama for treating PTSD in individuals undergoing substance use disorders. The study revealed that even those individuals who observed others during psychodrama sessions experienced benefits by gaining emotional insights and a sense of connection.

D&P have been shown to inspire audiences toward social change. Recent research shows that both performing and experiencing a performance can have positive effects on individuals, including the improvement of empathy and well-being by attending a traditional play or participating in interactive workshops, as exemplified by Rathje, Hackel, and Zaki (2021). This study examined how attending a live performance, the play Skeleton Crew, improved empathy, socio-political attitudes, and pro-social behaviors. The play focuses on the challenges faced by a group of auto workers in Detroit during the 2008 recession as they faced the threat that the factory where they work may close. The research found that audiences felt more empathy for factory workers and developed a greater concern for helping others. This is a good example of social contagion.

Interactive D&P also have been shown to influence institutional change. Workshops simulating real-life scenarios, such as how university faculty are hired, have been shown to help abate gender bias, for example, among faculty and administrators who might be on search committees (Shea et al., 2019). Following these workshops, 90 percent of participants reported increased awareness of biases, something that could only happen when people can empathize with the challenges women face in the job market. These findings show the potential for D&P-based interventions as vehicles for cultivating diversity and inclusivity in institutional settings, such as colleges and universities.

CONCLUSION

In *Freire and Drama—Marília: A Play,* I made connections between key concepts developed by Paulo Freire (*Pedagogy of the Oppressed*) and Augusto Boal (*Theatre of the Oppressed*) and the idea that art forms can be used successfully to spark reflection and action toward liberation. I showed that Bárbara Santos also has provided the needed reconceptualization of key concepts related to oppression to foster gender and sexual orientation pluralities. I showed how Freire's and Boal's theoretical concepts have given me, and many others, the tools to create theatrical vehicles in the form of drama and performance aimed at broadcasting personal experiences of self-determination and liberatory action to decolonizing white, heterosexual patriarchy. However, all tools that could be used against white, heterosexual patriarchy have been under attack by the Trump administration, domestically and globally. Funding streams for the use, study, and dissemination of anti-oppression tools—including factual news and information and social and cultural programs—have been shut down. The Corporation for Public Broadcasting, created by the US Congress in 1967 to oversee the federal government's investment in public television and radio had been severely crippled by budget cuts, six months into the second Trump administration. The administration has also issued executive orders to dismantle DEI initiatives across the federal government, federal contractors, and educational institutions.

Having used tools created by the oppressors to address oppression—e.g., funding for social and cultural programs and student loan programs that entangle students for decades—those of us fighting oppression in the United States are grappling with a new reality in which the President has established mechanisms for extortion, such as the elimination of funding in exchange of silence and repudiation of diversity, equity, and inclusion (DEI) of marginalized people in mainstream society. What Audre Lorde stated in 1970s has proven true: "The master's tools will never dismantle the master's house" (Lorde, 1979, pgs. 110–14).

I believe that the *Theatre of the Oppressed* resonates with Lorde, as its practices and techniques do not require the expensive trappings—auditoriums, sets, costumes, etc.—of traditional theater. I do not suggest that *Theatre of the Oppressed* does not need funding; but, as an anti-oppression tool, *Theatre of the Oppressed* has grown exponentially in the past fifty years precisely because it focuses on developing human curiosity and creativity without dependence on government funding, which, in the United States, is currently under the control of an aspiring dictator who would cripple anti-oppression efforts.

Following my personal and professional experiences now, in this current sociopolitical moment, in this book, I have focused specifically on how autobiographical content can be used in performance to tell stories about the lives and conflicts of real people. As an example, I shared my solo play, *Marília,* in which I explore the premature death of my sister, how a poor family dealt with such loss during the years of the dictatorship in Brazil, and my decision to immigrate to the United States at the end of the dictatorship. In *Marília,* I explore Freire's theoretical approaches and Boal's theatrical practices and communicate with Santos's intersectional approach to make sense of my life as a gender nonconforming, queer, poor immigrant who is currently a distinguished professor at a prestigious American university.

First, I present *Marília* to show how drama and performance can be used to pinpoint and criticize the oppressor's negative messages that those of us with marginalized and minoritized social identities must endure during our lifetime. Then, in Part II, Chapter 1, I introduced how xenophobia, racism, homophobia, transphobia, and poverty contribute to overall oppression and internalization of oppressive messages. I used passages from *Marília* to show the usefulness of dramatic text and performance to promote critical reflections on these issues. In the Appendix, I include two workshops that can be used among groups of readers and/or viewers of *Marília* to inspire critical action.

In Chapter 2, I discussed how Freire's, Boal's, and Santos's anti-oppression methods are interconnected and how they can be supported through drama and performance in any sociopolitical and economic environment at any given time. I showed how critical consciousness, the core of Freire's work, has formed the foundation that has advanced liberation by inspiring people across the globe to engage in personal and collective action against oppression and prejudice. I explored how the development of critical consciousness relies on art forms to help marginalized people participate in critical dialogues aimed at facilitating a process of critical reflection about oppressive forces and prejudices affecting people's lives.

After establishing the basic concepts of *Theatre of the Oppressed*, in Chapter 3, I expanded on the usefulness of drama and performance as vehicles to spark critical dialogues, as well as both reflection and action toward liberation. I focused on self-referential or autobiographical material as the essence of both *Pedagogy of the Oppressed* and *Theatre of the Oppressed* as they represent the voices of real people sharing their life experiences, perceptions, feelings, attitudes, opinions, certainties, and doubts. I made a case for solo performers to use autobiographical material to invite their audiences into an intimate space that encourages cooperation and social contagion, processes that foster audience members' empathy for the performer and one another.

Building on the concept of cooperation and social contagion, in Chapter 4, I summarized key pieces of evidence, both theoretical and empirical, to show how drama and performance have been and can be used to decrease oppression by cultivating audience members' empathy for one another and by helping audiences to develop new knowledge and attitudes more conducive to their own well-being. Here and in previous chapters, I provided several examples from various places across the globe to describe the potential for art forms in general and drama and performance to change the status quo that insists on privileging white, heterosexual patriarchy.

As expressed in the Introduction, *Freire and Drama—Marília: A Play* is not all-inclusive, nor is it intended to provide definitive proof of how and why drama and performance are helpful in the fight against oppression and prejudice. Every idea that I expressed here is my own, and they are based on literature that has limitations. Nonetheless, these limitations pale in the face of the evidence that has been produced by a global movement against oppression and pro-liberation. There is no doubt that the outcomes associated with the arts and their benefits, for example, in cultivating empathy and well-being, have not been fully demonstrated in experimental research, which is considered the "gold standard" in research. I contend that this notion of a "gold standard" is in and of itself a form of oppression that privileges the perspectives of a white, heterosexual, patriarchal society.

I also wish to admonish against critiques that aim at parsing out the definition of "art" or what art is and what it is not. I believe that we need a broad definition of art that encompasses what myriad cultures across the globe have defined, loved, and lived as art and how different cultures have developed their own arts-based interventions. A broad and global understanding is in and of itself a tool against any white, heterosexual patriarchal assertion of what art is or what it can and cannot do. It is also true that reports on the impact of the myriad art forms that we know thus far must be accurate. Reports on arts-based interventions need to be clearly described, and their usefulness not over-stated.

It is important to note that drama and performance on stage and/or in other public spaces are not available equally or equitably across the globe. As we think about using live drama and performance, we also need to think of accessibility in all ways possible, from how much it costs to who can physically access it to who is sponsoring it. We also need to account for the fact that drama and performance may be limited in their abilities to improve reflection and action among audiences who already agree with the worldviews being presented. Therefore, it is important to create opportunities that question existing beliefs to develop new ones. I believe my play *Marília* serves as an example of how boundaries related to sexual molestation, poverty, racism, and other forms of oppression can be expanded within the same drama and performance.

Freire and Drama—Marília: A Play provides a vision for using autobiographical material to support critical dialogues about socioeconomic and political issues taking place worldwide by using the Brazilian dictatorship (1964–85) as the context for *Marília*. The play has been performed several times, engaging audiences from all walks of life living in different social contexts. I hope it will engage theater-makers and theatergoers in the process of research, practice, and scholarship to advance our understanding of the connections that exist between art and liberation. At this moment, December 2025, as I write this last paragraph, in the United States, we are facing perhaps the widest in scope and deepest moment of political repression and hatred under the Trump regime. The regime has expressly and openly declared its plan and actions to destroy all advances that have been made thus far toward DEI. Let this moment be met with global resistance that will use all the tools available to us to combat it at home and stop it from taking place elsewhere. Cutting-edge artistic research and practices, particularly those that include drama and performance, might be the very tools that we need to fight against oppression and prejudice to be liberated.

APPENDIX

This appendix includes instructions for two workshops (about 60 minutes each) created in collaboration with Marc Arthur in 2021. Both workshops can be used among groups of readers and/or viewers of *Marília* to inspire discussion and action. Encouraging students to perform short monologues is highly encouraged. The workshops offer practical exercises that optimize learning and reflection, both of which are known to raise critical consciousness.

In *Marília*, I expound on my work experiences in the United States, first as a poor immigrant and later as a hairdresser. I also explored several moments in which I felt like I was my sister, or my dead sister was inside me, helping me face and cope with difficult circumstances. The embodiment of these experiences will help participants to (1) practice improvisational and cooperative empathy and (2) develop listening and empathy skills around issues concerning poverty, grief, xenophobia, racism, homophobia, and transphobia. These activities will foster an inclusive environment drawing on the autobiographical themes present in *Marília*.

Workshop # 1: "The Hairdresser"

Objectives

This workshop will help participants to (1) practice improvisational and collaborative empathy and (2) develop listening and empathy skills around issues concerning poverty, grief, xenophobia, racism, homophobia, and transphobia.

Warm-Up Steps

1   Without talking or contacting, participants walk around the space. The goal is for participants to become aware of space and how their bodies occupy space.

2   They are asked to fill in any empty space and move faster.

3   The group facilitator calls "freeze" and everyone reflects on where they are in the space.

4   This exercise is repeated with different tempos of movement three times.

5   While participants are moving quickly, they are asked to stop next to one person.

6   This person becomes a partner for the exercise that follows.

Exercise

1   Working in pairs, each person selects who will play a hairdresser or the client.

2   The client tells a short narrative about an experience (fictional or real, depending on comfort level) they had, such as poverty, grief, xenophobia, racism, homophobia, and transphobia.

3   The client sits in a chair, and the hairdresser stands behind, pretending to cut or treat their hair.

4   The client tells a story (fictional or real, depending on comfort level), perhaps the revelation of a secret.

5   The hairdresser does not speak; only listens and then restates the narrative and words of empathy.

6   Switch roles and do the exercise again.

Recommendations for Optimal Pedagogical Impact

- The narrative need not be more than 5 minutes long.

- Participants should share narratives as something that they are revealing for the first time.

- Participants are encouraged to think about how they feel as they share their stories.

- The hairdresser should focus on listening deeply to be able to repeat it back in detail.

- Participants are encouraged to make the human connection between them to be as real as possible.

Questions for Discussion

- What were the key topics spoken about? Please describe them.

- What was difficult to hear? Anything taboo? What felt normal?

- Given the issues explored by the hairdresser and client, what details or feelings about the situation did not come up? Any ideas why?

- What were some of the patterns across different scenes portrayed by different pairs?

- How did it feel to listen deeply and speak?

Recommendations for Facilitators

- Facilitators are encouraged to engage with any content brought up during the performances.

- Ask participants to be open to the wide array of life experiences and feelings human beings share.

- Add questions that might be pertinent to specific groups of participants and social contexts.

- Ask participants to suspend judgments for the duration of the workshop and to speak with the facilitator after the workshop, in case there might be issues for which they need privacy to discuss.

- Ask participants to identify the usefulness of different media (e.g., drama, music, sculpture) that can be integrated into social justice practice and self-healing.

- Ask participants to evaluate how specific art forms and practices can support liberation in different socioeconomic and political contexts.

Workshop # 2: "A Marília Moment"

Objectives

"A Marília Moment" refers to moments that the protagonist in *Marília* must face and cope with difficult situations concerning poverty, grief, xenophobia, racism, homophobia, and transphobia. In these moments, the protagonist seeks help from his dead sister to regain and restore well-being. This workshop will help participants embody a gesture or a characteristic of someone who has passed away (or is still alive) and on whom they may have relied.

Warm-Up Steps

1   Ask the group to form a circle.

2   Ask each person to say their name. Continue until each person knows everyone's name.

3   Ask a volunteer to walk across the room and then ask the group to describe the person's walk.

4   Ask the volunteer to walk again across the room, this time "showing" the purpose of the walk. What were they trying to convey with the walk?

5   Ask the group to describe what were the differences between "walking" and "showing the walk."

Exercise: Part 1

1   Give participants a "trigger warning" before asking them to find a place in the room and, sit comfortably and close their eyes.

2   Ask them to imagine a friend, relative, or pet who has died or to choose an object that is special to them and which they lost or was stolen from them.

3   Ask participants to "embody" that person, pet, or object by using voice/sound, physical characteristics, and scents and by thinking of physical gestures or shapes of objects that reflect those memories.

4   Start with small movements of hands, feet, head, and so on.

5   After about 3 minutes, ask everyone to pick one movement and practice it.

6 Ask everyone to open their eyes and form a circle again.

7 Go around the circle and ask participants to perform the gesture they focused on.

Exercise: Part 2

1 Ask participants to partner up with the person next to them and find a place in the room to have a conversation about the gestures they used previously.

2 Ask them to discuss the following questions: (1) What did you experience during the process of embodying your person or object? (2) What felt good? (3) What was challenging? (4) Does the final gesture you performed for the group reflect the culture you were brought up in? How so?

3 After this conversation, instruct each pair to take turns telling a story about how they had "A Marília Moment"—when their relative or friend enabled them or changed their perspective in some way.

Questions for Discussion

- What felt most vulnerable and most empowering?

- What came up during the conversation with partners?

- How did it feel to reflect and listen?

- What similarities were there in terms of how each person experienced the loss?

- What differences, if any, might there be when the loss is that of a person, pet, or object?

- How did your memory of something/someone that was lost reflect (or not) empathy and well-being in your life?

Recommendations for Facilitators

- Follow recommendations from the previous workshop, plus the following.

- Offer a trigger warning, allowing participants to opt-out if desired.

- Guide participants by offering advice, such as "Think of how this person moved," "How do you remember them?"

- If participants get lost or their conversations end early, instruct them to continue practicing and refining the gestures that embody someone, pet, or object that is no longer in their lives.

BIBLIOGRAPHY

Adams, T., & Holman Jones, S. (2011). Telling stories: Reflexivity, queer theory, and autoethnography. *Cultural Studies–Critical Methodologies*, 11(2), 108–16. Doi: 10.1177/1532708611401329.

Anthias, F. (2008). Thinking through the lens of translocational positionality: An intersectionality frame for understanding identity and belonging. *Translocations*, 4(1), 5–20.

Arandjelović, O. (2023). The making of a discriminatory ism. *Equality, Diversity and Inclusion: An International Journal*, 42(8), 1038–50.

Austin, A. (2016). "There I am": A grounded theory study of young adults navigating a transgender or gender nonconforming identity within a context of oppression and invisibility. *Sex Roles: A Journal of Research*, 75(506), 215–30.

Austin, A., & Goodman, R. (2017). The impact of social connectedness and internalized transphobic stigma on self-esteem among transgender and gender non-conforming adults. *Journal of Homosexuality*, 64(6), 825–41.

Bacouël, A. S., Shantz, A., & Bacouël-Jentjens (2024). An artful workplace of the future: The role of art-based interventions in fostering levers for creativity among a diverse workforce. *European Management Review*. http://dx.doi.org/10.1111/emre.12680.

Baer, P., Salisbury, J., & Goldstein, T. (2019). *Pairing verbatim theatre and theatre of the oppressed to provoke startling empathy*. West Lafayette, IN: Routledge.

Bandini, E., & Maggi, M. (2014). Transphobia. In Corona, G., Jannini, E. A., & Maggi, M. (Eds.), *Emotional, physical and sexual abuse: Impact in children and social minorities* (pp. 49–59). Springer International Publishing.

Barak, A. (2016). Critical consciousness in critical social work: Learning from the theatre of the oppressed. *British Journal of Social Work*, 46(6), 1776–92. https://doi.org/10.1093/bjsw/bcv102.

Bernal-Munera, M. (2023). *A social justice biology curriculum to strengthen community college students' critical consciousness* (Masters thesis, University of Illinois Chicago). https://doi.org/10.25417/uic.25392820.v1.

Boal, A. (1985). *Theatre of the oppressed.* New York: Theater Communications Group.

Boal, A. (1993). *Theatre of the oppressed.* New York: Theatre Communications Group.

Boal, A. (2006). *Aesthetics of the oppressed.* London and New York: Routledge.

Bockting, W. O., Miner, M. H., Swinburne Romine, R. E., Dolezal, C., Robinson, B. B. E., Rosser, B. S., & Coleman, E. (2020). The transgender identity survey: A measure of internalized transphobia. *LGBT Health*, 7(1), 15–27.

Brondolo, E., Libretti, M., Rivera, L., & Walsemann, K. M. (2012). Racism and social capital: The implications for social and physical well-being. *Journal of Social Issues*, 68(2), 358–84.

Carlson, E. D., Engebretson, J., & Chamberlain, R. M. (2006). Photovoice as a social process of critical consciousness. *Qualitative Health Research*, 16(6), 836–52. http://dx.doi.org/10.1177/1049732306287525.

Centers for Disease Control and Prevention (2004). About emotional well-being. U.S. Department of Health and Human Services. https://www.cdc.gov/emotional-well-being/about/.

Cervantes-Soon, C. G., Dorner, L., Palmer, D., Heiman, D., Schwerdtfeger, R., & Choi, J. (2017). Combating inequalities in two-way language immersion programs: Toward critical consciousness in bilingual education spaces. *Review of Research in Education*, 41(1), 403–27. https://doi-org.proxy.lib.umich.edu/10.3102/0091732X17690120.

Chavis, A., & Johnson, D. (2023). Internalized racism and racial self-identity formation in Black children. *Pediatrics*, 152(2), e2023061292.

Chin, M. H., Orlov, N. M., Callender, B. C., Dolan, J. A., Miller, D. C., Peek, M. E., Rusiecki, J. M., & Vela, M. B. (2023). Improvisational and standup comedy, graphic medicine, and theatre of the oppressed to teach advancing health equity. *Academic Medicine*, 97(12), 1732–7.

Corsa, A. J. (2020). Empathy and moral education, Theatre of the Oppressed, and The Laramie Project. *Journal of Moral*

Education, 50(2), 219–32. https://doi.org/10.1080/03057240.20 19.1703658.

Cronin, T. J., Pepping, C. A., & Lyons, A. (2019). Internalized transphobia and well-being: The moderating role of attachment. *Personality and Individual Differences*, 143, 80–3.

Dabène, O. (2020). *Street art and democracy in Latin America*. London: Springer Nature. https://link.springer.com/ book/10.1007/978-3-030-26913-5.

David, E. J. R. (Ed.) (2013). *Internalized oppression: The psychology of marginalized groups*. New York: Springer Publishing Company.

David, E. J. R., Schroeder, T. M., & Fernandez, J. (2019). Internalized racism: A systematic review of the psychological literature on racism's most insidious consequence. *Journal of Social Issues*, 75(4), 1057–86. https://doi.org/10.1111/josi.12350.

Devulsky, A. (2021). *Colorismo*. São Paulo: Jandaira.

DiAngelo, R. (1997). Heterosexism: Addressing internalized dominance. *Journal of Progessive Human Services*, 8(1), 5–21.

Dinsmore, C. (1991). *From surviving to thriving: Incest, feminism, and recovery*. New York: State University of New York Press.

Dunne, P. (2016). Restoried script performance. In Pendzik, S., Emunah, R., & Johson, D. R. (Eds.), *The self in performance: Context, definitions, directions*. New York: Palgrave Macmillan.

Dworking, Shari L. (2005). Who is epidemiologically fathomable in the HIV/AIDS epidemic? Gender, sexuality, and intersectionality in public health. *Culture, Health & Sexuality* 7, 615–23.

Dziwa, D. D., Postma, L., & Combrink, L. (2022). Transcending gender dichotomy through art teacher education in Zimbabwe. *International Journal of Education Through Art*, 18(1), 33–49. https://doi.org/10.1386/eta_00081_1.

Emunah, R. (2015). Self-revelatory performance: A form of drama therapy and theater. *Drama Therapy Review*, 1(1), 71–85.

Emunah, R. (2020). *Acting for real: Drama therapy process, technique, and performance* (2nd ed.). New York and London: Routledge, Taylor and Francis Group.

Fancourt, D., & Finn, S. (2019). What is the evidence on the role of the arts in improving health and well-being? A scoping review. *Health Evidence Network Synthesis Report, No. 67*. Copenhagen: WHO Regional Office for Europe.

Fantus, S. (2020). Teaching note—Theatre of the oppressed and social work ethics education: An innovative teaching module. *Journal of Social Work Education*, 56(3), 607–13.

Federal Bureau of Investigation (2019). *Incidents and offenses. 2019 Hate crime statistics*. Uniform Crime Reporting. https://ucr.fbi.gov/hate-crime/2019/topic-pages/incidents-and-offenses.

Fiddian-Green, A., Kim, S., Gubrium, A. C., Larkey, L., & Peterson, J. C. (2019). Restor(y)ing health: A conceptual model of the effects of digital storytelling. *Health Promotion Practice*, 20(4), 502–12. https://doi.org/10.1177/1524839918825130.

Flentje, A., Heck, N. C., Brennan, J. M., & Meyer, I. H. (2020). The relationship between minority stress and biological outcomes: A systematic review. *Journal of Behavioral Medicine*, 43(5), 673–94.

Fox, H., & Leeder, A. (2015). *Combining theatre of the oppressed, playback theatre, and autobiographical theatre for social action in higher education. Theatre topics*. Baltimore, MD: Johns Hopkins University Press.

Freire, P. (2000). *Pedagogy of the oppressed* (30th anniversary ed.). London and New York: Continuum Publishing and Bloomsbury.

Frost, D. M., & Meyer, I. H. (2023). Minority stress theory: Application, critique, and continued relevance. *Current Opinion in Psychology*, 51. https://doi.org/10.1016/j.copsyc.2023.101579.

Frye, V., Paige, M. Q., Gordon, S., Matthews, D., Musgrave, G., Greene, E., Kornegay, M., Farhat, D., Smith, P. H., Usher, D., Phelan, J. C., Koblin, B. A., & Taylor-Akutagawa, V. (2019). Impact of a community-level intervention on HIV stigma, homophobia and HIV testing in New York City: Results from project CHHANGE. *Stigma and Health*, 4(1), 72–81.

Garcia, B., Crifasi, E., & Dessel, A. (2019). Oppression pedagogy: Intergroup dialogue and theatre of the oppressed in creating a safe enough classroom. *Journal of Social Work Education*, 55(4), 669–83.

Gay, G., & Kirkland, K. (2003). Developing cultural critical consciousness and self-reflection in preservice teacher education. *Theory into Practice*, 42(3), 181–7. http://www.jstor.org/stable/1477418.

Giacomucci, S., & Marquit, J. (2020). The effectiveness of trauma-focused psychodrama in the treatment of PTSD in inpatient substance abuse treatment. *Frontiers in Psychology*, 11, 896. https://doi.org/10.3389/fpsyg.2020.00896.

Gibbons, P., & Fiske, S. T. (1999). A child dies, a child survives: The impact of sibling loss. *Journal of Pediatric Health Care*, 6(2), 65–72.

Giesler, M. A. (2017). Teaching note-theatre of the oppressed and social work education: Radicalizing the practice classroom. *Journal of Social Work Education*, 53(2), 347–53.

Glick, P., & Fiske, S. T. (1999). Sexism and other "isms": Independence, status, and the ambivalent content of stereotypes. In Swann, W. B., Jr., Langlois, J. H., & Gilbert, L. A. (Eds.), *Sexism and stereotypes in modern society: The gender sciene of Janet Taylor Spence* (pp. 193–221). Washington, DC: American Psychological Association.

Goffman, E. (1959). *The presentation of self in everyday life*. Garden City, New York: Anchor/Doubleday.

Haddad, S., & Di Pierro, M. C. (2021). Considerations on popular education and adults schooling in the thought and practice of Paulo Freire. SEÇÃO COMEMORATIVA | PAULO FREIRE 100 ANOS, ENSAIO • Educ. Soc. 42.https://doi.org/10.1590/ ES.255872.

Harrell, S. P. (2000). A multidimensional conceptualization of racism-related stress: Implications for the well-being of people of color. *American Journal of Orthopsychiatry*, 70(1), 42–57.

Haushofer, J., & Fehr, E. (2014). On the psychology of poverty. *Science*, 344(6186), 862–7.

Heberle, A. E., Rapa, L. J., & Farago, F. (2020). Critical consciousness in children and adolescents: A systematic review, critical assessment, and recommendations for future research. *Psychological Bulletin*, 146(6), 525–51. https://doi.org/10.1037/ bul0000230.

Heddon, D. (2008). *Autobiography and performance*. Hampshire and New York: Palgrave Macmillan.

Herek, G. M. (2004). Beyond "homophobia": Thinking about sexual prejudice and stigma in the twenty-first century. *Sexuality Research & Social Policy: A Journal of the NSRC*, 1(2), 6–24.

Hitchcock, J. (2002). *Lifting the white veil: An exploration of White American culture in a multicultural context*. Roselle, NJ: Crandall, Dostie, and Douglass Books.

Honikman, S., Field, S., & Cooper, S. (2019). The secret history method and the development of an ethos of care: Preparing the maternity environment for integrating mental health care

in South Africa. *Transcultural Psychiatry*, 57(1). https://doi.
org/10.1177/1363461519844640.

Hoy-Ellis, C. P. (2023). Minority stress and mental health: A review
of the literature. *Journal of Homosexuality*, 70(5), 806–30.

Huebner, D. M., McGarrity, L. A., Perry, N. S., Spivey, L. A., &
Smith, T. W. (2021). Cardiovascular and cortisol responses to
experimentally-induced minority stress. *Health Psychology*,
40(5), 316–25.

Huppert, F. A., & So, T. T. C. (February 2013). Flourishing across
Europe: Application of a new conceptual framework for defining
well-being. *Social Indicators Research*, 110(3), 837–861. doi:
10.1007/s11205-011-9966-7. Epub 2011 Dec 15. PMID:
23329863; PMCID: PMC3545194.

Jeffries, W. L. IV, Marks, G., Lauby, J., Murrill, C. S., & Millett, G.
A. (2013). Homophobia is associated with sexual behavior that
increases risk of acquiring and transmitting HIV infection among
Black men who have sex with men. *AIDS and Behavior* 17(4),
1442–53.

Jemal, A., & Bussey, S. (2018). Transformative action: A theoretical
framework for breaking new ground. *EJournal of Public Affairs*,
7(2), 37–65.

Jones, E. E., & Pitman, T. S. (1982). Toward a general theory
of strategic self-presentation. In Suls, J. (Ed.), *Psychological
perspectives on the self* (pp. 257–78). New York: Sage
Publications.

Jones, K. P., Sabat, I. E., King, E. B., Ahmad, A., McCausland, T.
C., & Chen, T. (2017). Isms and schisms: A meta-analysis of the
prejudice-discrimination relationship across racism, sexism, and
ageism. *Journal of Organizational Behavior*, 38(7), 1076–110.

Kardec, A. (2020). *The gospel according to spiritism* (1st ed.,
trans. from original 1866). New York: United States Spiritist
Federation.

Keisari, S., Palgi, Y., Yaniv, D., & Gesser-Edelsburg, A. (2020).
Participation in life-review playback theater enhances mental
health of community-dwelling older adults: A randomized
controlled trial. *Journal of Aging Studies*, 58, 100873. https://doi.
org/10.1037/aca0000354.

Kohrt, A., Ottman, K., Panter-Brick, C., Konner, M., & Patel, V.
(2020). Why we heal: The evolution of psychological healing

and implications for global mental health. *Clinical Psychology Review*, 82, 101920. https://doi.org/10.1016/j.cpr.2020.101920.

Kronenfeld, D. B., Bennardo, G., De Munck, V. C., & Fischer, M. D. (Eds.) (2015). *A companion to cognitive anthropology*. New Jersey: John Wiley & Sons/Blackwell Publishing.

Kumagai, A. K., & Lypson, M. L. (2009). Beyond cultural competence: Critical consciousness, social justice, and multicultural education. *Academic Medicine*, 84(6), 782–7. Doi: 10.1097/ACM.0b013e3181a42398.

Lewis, T. E. (2012). Teaching with pensive images: Rethinking curiosity in Paulo Freire's pedagogy of the oppressed. *The Journal of Aesthetic Education*, 46(1), 27–45. https://www.jstor.org/stable/10.5406/jaesteduc.46.1.0027.

Liu, C., Xie, Y., Xu, Y., Song, Z., Tang, J., Shen, J., Jiang, Z., Shen, C., Zhan, X., & Zheng, C. (2024). Assessing the stress-relief impact of an art-based intervention inspired by the broaden-and-build theory in college students. *Frontiers in Psychology*, 15, 1324415. https://doi.org/10.3389/fpsyg.2024.1324415.

Lorde, A. (1979). The master's tools will never dismantle the master's house. In N. K. Bereano (Ed.), *Sister outsider: Essays and speeches* (2007 Edition, pp. 110–14). Ed. Berkeley, CA: Crossing Press.

Lüthi, E., Pichonnaz, L., Schwarz, J., Morier-Genoud, P., Dayer, C., Rrustemi, I., Schilter, L., Berney, A., John, C., Dubois, J., Rodondi, P. Y., & Clair, C. (2022). Preventing sexism and sexual harassment in medical schools by using theater of the oppressed as an interactive and reflexive tool. *BMC Research Notes*, 15(1), 192. https://doi.org/10.1186/s13104-022-06084-2.

Markman, E. R. (2011). Gender identity disorder, the gender binary, and transgender oppression: Implications for ethical social work. *Smith College Studies in Social Work*, 81(4), 314–27.

McConnell, E. A., Janulis, P., Phillips II, G., Truong, R., & Birkett, M. (2018). Multiple minority stress and LGBT community resilience among sexual minority men. *Psychology of Sexual Orientation and Gender Diversity*, 5(1), 1–12.

Mernick, A. (2021). Critical arts pedagogy: Nurturing critical consciousness and self-actualization through art education. *Art Education*, 74(5), 19–24. https://doi.org/10.1080/00043125.2021.1928468.

Mizock, L., & Mueser, K. T. (2014). Employment, mental health, internalized stigma, and coping with transphobia among transgender individuals. *Psychology of Sexual Orientation and Gender Diversity*, 1(2), 146–8.

Motta-Ochoa, R., Patenaude, D., Barbe-Welzel, M. A., Incio-Serra, N., Audeoud, E. R., Gómez-Rendón, A., & Flores-Aranda, J. (2024). Evidence about art-based interventions for indigenous people: A scoping review protocol. *BMJ Open*, 14(6), e083448. https://doi.org/10.1136/bmjopen-2023-083448.

Oepen, R., & Gruber, H. (2024). Art-based interventions and art therapy to promote health of migrant populations: A systematic literature review of current research. *Arts & Health*, 16(3), 266–284. https://doi.org/10.1080/17533015.2023.2252003.

Ozga, K. A. (2016). Effects of photography-based public art on the school environment. *Studies in Art Education*, 57(3), 203–20. https://doi.org/10.1080/00393541.2016.1177365.

Padilla, L. M. (2001). But you're not a dirty Mexican: Internalized oppression, Latinos & law. *Texas Hispanic Journal of Law & Policy*, 7, 59–114.

Pavlidis, P. (2015). Social consciousness, education and transformative activity. *Journal for Critical Education Policy Studies*, 13(2), 1–37.

Perkins, R., Mason-Bertrand, A., Tymoszuk, U., Spiro, N., Gee, K., & Williamon, A. (2021). Arts engagement supports social connectedness in adulthood: Findings from the HEartS Survey. *BMC Public Health*, 21(1), 1208. https://doi.org/10.1186/s12889-021-11233-6.

Pheterson, G. (1986). Alliances between women: Overcoming internalized oppression and internalized domination. *Signs: Journal of Women in Culture and Society*, 12(1), 146–60.

Pinkney, C. (2014). The effects of internalized oppression on the Black community. *Stylus Knights Write Showcase*, 94–100.

Pinto, R. M. (2022a). Autoethnographic playwriting and performance for self-healing and advocacy. In Huss, E., & Bos, E. (Eds.), *Social work research using arts-based methods* (pp. 45–54). UK: Policy Press/Bristol University Press.

Pinto, R. M. (2022b). Autoethnographic playwriting and performance to research immigration, marginalized gender identities, and loss. In Huss, E., & Bos, E. (Eds.), *Social work research using arts-based methods* (pp. 45–54). United Kingdom: Policy Press/Bristol University Press.

Pinto, R. M. (2022c). Realm of the dead: A mixed-media installation performance. *Ground Works*. https://groundworks.io/journal. © 2022 by Rogério Meireles Pinto is licensed under CC-BY-NC-ND 4.0. https://doi.org/10.48807/2022.0.0105.

Pinto, R. M., Melendez, R. M., & Spector, A. Y. (2008). Male-to-female transgender individuals building social support and capital from within a gender-focused network. *Journal of Gay & Lesbian Social Services Issues in Practice, Policy & Research*, 20(3), 203–20.

Pinto, R. M., Lee, C. A., Arthur, M., & Windsor, L. C. (2024a). Iconic illustrations initiate critical dialogues among heterosexual men who then develop critical consciousness around homophobia and sexism: A qualitative study. *Sexual and Gender Diversity in Social Services*, 37(1), 116–40. https://doi.org/10.108 0/29933021.2024.2354358.

Pinto, R. M., Windsor, L., & Benoit, E. (2024b). Participation in critical dialogues with illustrative images increases knowledge about COVID-19 prevention: A mixed methods longitudinal approach. *Journal of Mixed Methods Research*, 18(3), 304–17. https://journals.sagepub.com/eprint/ VSYTIVMA5JADNFPHUZKE/full.

Pinto, R. M., Im, V., Lee, C., Hall, E., Bonnewit, I., Granillo, E., & Windsor, L. (accepted). Critical dialogues sparked by painted images faciliate critical consciousness among formerly incarcerated men: An exploratory study. *Journal of Social Work Practice in the Addictions*.

Ramirez, J. L., & Paz Galupo, M. (2019). Multiple minority stress: The role of proximal and distal stress on mental health outcomes among lesbian, gay, and bisexual people of color. *Journal of Gay & Lesbian Mental Health*, 23(2), 145–67.

Rathje, S., Hackel, L., & Zaki, J. (2021). Attending live theatre improves empathy, changes attitudes, and leads to pro-social behavior. *Journal of Experimental Social Psychology*, 95, 104138. https://doi.org/10.1016/j.jesp.2021.104138.

Ray, P., & Pendzik, S. (2021). Autobiographical therapeutic performance as a means of improving executive functioning in traumatized adults. *Frontiers in Psychology*, 12, 599914. https:// doi.org/10.3389/fpsyg.2021.599914.

Rood, B. A., Reisner, S. L., Puckett, J. A., Surace, F. I., Berman, A. K., & Pantalone, D. W. (2017). Internalized transphobia: Exploring perceptions of social messages in transgender and gender-nonconforming adults. *International Journal of Transgenderism*, 18(4), 411–26.

Rothenberg, P. S. (2004). *Race, class, and gender in the United States: An integrated study*. London & New York: Macmillan Publishers.

Rumbaut, R. G. (2015). Assimilation of immigrants. In Wright, J. D. (Ed.), *International Encyclopedia of the Social & Behavioral Sciences*, vol. 2 (pp. 81–7). Oxford: Elsevier.

Saeed, H. (2015). Empowering unheard voices through "Theatre of the Oppressed": Reflections on the legislative theatre project for women in Afghanistan, notes from the field. *Journal of Human Rights Practice*, 7(2). http://dx.doi.org/10.1093/jhuman/huu028.

Saldãna, J. (2003). Dramatizing data: A premier. *Qualitative Inquiry*, 9(2), 218–36. https://doi.org/10.1177/1077800402250932.

Santos, B. (2016). *Teatro do oprimido: Raízes e asas: Uma Teoria da práxis*. Rio de Janeiro: Ibis Libris.

Santos, B. (2023). *Teatro das Oprimidas: Feminist aesthetics for political poetics*. São Paulo: Casa Philos.

Scandurra, C., Bochicchio, V., Amodeo, A. L., Esposito, C., Valerio, P., Maldonato, N. M., Bacchini, D., & Vitelli, R. (2018). Internalized transphobia, resilience, and mental health: Applying the psychological mediation framework to Italian transgender individuals. *International Journal of Environmental Research and Public Health*, 15(3), 508.

Schwenke, D., Dshemuchadse, M., Rasehorn, L., Klarhölter, D., & Scherbaum, S. (2020). Improv to improve: The impact of improvisational theater on creativity, acceptance, and psychological well-being. *Journal of Creativity in Mental Health*, 16(1), 31–48. https://doi.org/10.1080/15401383.2020.1754987.

Seligman, M. E. P. (2012). *Flourishing*. New York: Free Press.

Shain, A. (2005). Disability, theatre and power: An analysis of a one-person play. *Canadian Theatre Review*, 122, 13–18.

Shaked, E., Bensimon, M., & Tuval Mashiach, R. (2021). Internalization and opposition to stigmatized social discourse among incest survivors. *Journal of Child Sexual Abuse*, 30(7), 847–68.

Shea, C. M., Malone, M. F. F. T., Young, J. R., & Graham, K. J. (2019). Interactive theater: An effective tool to reduce gender bias in faculty searches. *Equality, Diversity and Inclusion*, 38(2), 178–87. https://doi.org/10.1108/EDI-09-2017-0187.

Sheehy-Skeffington, J., & Rea, J. (2017). *How poverty affects people's decision-making processes*. London: School of Economics and Political Science.

Shin, R. Q., Smith, L. C., Lu, Y., Welch, J. C., Sharma, R., Vernay, C. N., & Yee, S. (2018). The development and validation of the contemporary critical consciousness measure II. *Journal of Counseling Psychology*, 65(5), 539–55.

Siberz, P. (2009). When one is enough: The one-person play [*Senior Theses*, Linfield University]. https://digitalcommons.linfield.edu/dcestud_theses/2.

Snyder, T. (2017). *On tyranny: Twenty lessons from the twentieth century*. New York: Crow.

Soots, L. (2015). Flourishing. *The Positive Psychology People*. Retrieved from http://www.thepositivepsychologypeople.com/flourishing.

Speer, S. A. (2015). Responding to-isms. *Journal of Language and Social Psychology*, 34(4), 464–70.

Spry, T. (2010). Call it swing: A jazz blues autoethnography. *Cultural Studies–Critical Methodologies*, 10(4), 271–82.

Stephan, M., Register, J., Reinke, L., Robinson, C., Pugalenthi, P., & Pugalee, D. (2021). People use math as a weapon: Critical mathematics consciousness in the time of COVID-19. *Educational Studies in Mathematics*, 108(3), 513–32. Doi: 10.1007/s10649-021-10062-z.

Sullivan, J., Petronella, S., Brooks, E., Murillo, M., Primeau, L., & Ward, J. (2008). Theatre of the oppressed and environmental justice communities: A transformational therapy for the body politic. *Journal of Health Psychology*, 13(2), 166–79.

Sundstrom, R. R., & Kim, D. H. (2014). Xenophobia and racism. *Critical Philosophy of Race*, 2(1), 20–45.

Tafira, K. (2011). Is xenophobia racism? *Anthropology Southern Africa*, 34(3–4), 114–21.

Tan, K. K. H, Treharne, G. J., Ellis, S. J., Schmidt, J. M., & Veale, J. F. (2020). Gender minority stress: A critical review. *Journal of Homosexuality*, 67(10), 1471–89.

Tang, S. X., Seelaus, K. H., Moore, T. M., Taylor, J., Moog, C., O'Connor, D., Burkholder, M., Kohler, C. G., Grant, P. M., Eliash, D., Calkins, M. E., Gur, R. E., & Gur, R. C. (2020). Theatre improvisation training to promote social cognition: A novel recovery-oriented intervention for youths at clinical risk for psychosis. *Early Intervention in Psychiatry*, 14(2), 163–71.

Tappan, M. B. (2006). Refraining internalized oppression and internalized domination: From the psychological to the sociocultural. *Teachers College Record*, 108(10), 2115–44.

Testoni, I., Tomasella, E., Pompele, S., Mascarin, M., & Wieser, M. A. (2020). Can desire and wellbeing be promoted in adolescents and young adults affected by cancer? Phototherapy as a mirror that increases resilience. *Frontiers in Psychology*, 11, 966. https://doi.org/10.3389/fpsyg.2020.00966.

Tochluk, S. (2013). "But I just don't see it!": Making white superiority visible. *Understanding and Dismantling Privilege*, 3(1), 1–21.

Ünal, E., & Erdoğan-Yüce, G. (2025). The effectiveness of art-based interventions for cancer patients: A systematic review and meta-analysis. *European Journal of Oncology Nursing*, 74, 102755. https://doi.org/10.1016/j.ejon.2024.102755.

Vacca, V. J. (1997). Telling women's lives: African-American one-person plays. *American Drama*, 6(2), 58.

van Bewer, V., Woodgate, R. L., Martin, D., & Deer, F. (2021). Exploring theatre of the oppressed and forum theatre as pedagogies in nursing education. *Nurse Education Today*, 103, 104940. https://doi.org/10.1016/j.nedt.2021.104940.

Wagle, U. (2002). Rethinking poverty: Definition and measurement. *International Social Science Journal*, 54(171), 155–65.

Wake, B. M. (2022). Service or saviorism: Deconstructing benevolent racism in the helping professions. In Johnson, K. F., Sparkman-Key, N. M., Meca, A., & Tarver, S. Z. (Eds.), *Developing anti-racist practices in the helping professions: Inclusive theory, pedagogy, and application* (pp. 93–110). Springer International Publishing.

Watts, J. W., & Abdul-Adil, J. K. (1998). Promoting critical consciousness in young, African-American men. *Journal of Prevention & Intervention*, 16(1–2), 63–86. Doi:10.1300/J005v16n01_04.

Watts, R. J., Abdul-Adil, J. K., & Pratt, T. (2002). Enhancing critical consciousness in young African American men: A psychoeducational approach. *Psychology of Men & Masculinity*, 3(1), 41–50. https://doi.org/10.1037/1524-9220.3.1.41.

Watts, R. J., Diemer, M. A., & Voight, A. M. (2011). Critical consciousness: Current status and future directions. *New Directions for Child and Adolescent Development*, 134, 43–57. https://doi.org/10.1002/cd.310.

Wilkerson, I. (2020). *Caste: The origins of our discontents*. New York: Random House.

Wynne, L. (2019). *Empowerment and the individualisation of resistance: A Foucauldian perspective on Theatre of the Oppressed*. Critical social policy. London: SAGE Publications.

Zorrilla, A., & Tisdell, E. J. (2016). Art as critical public pedagogy: A qualitative study of Luis Camnitzer and his conceptual art. *Adult Education Quarterly*, 66(3), 273–91. https://doi.org/10.1177/0741713616645666.

INDEX

Page numbers in italics refer to figures and tables.